AMERICAN PLAYBOOK

A GUIDE TO WINNING BACK
THE COUNTRY FROM THE DEMOCRATS

CLAY TRAVIS

THRESHOLD EDITIONS

NEW YORK LONDON TORONTO SYDNEY NEW DELHI

Threshold Editions
An Imprint of Simon & Schuster, Inc.
1230 Avenue of the Americas
New York, NY 10020

First Threshold Editions hardcover edition August 2023

THRESHOLD EDITIONS and colophon are trademarks of
Simon & Schuster, Inc.

For information about special discounts for bulk purchases,
please contact Simon & Schuster Special Sales at
1-866-506-1949 or business@simonandschuster.com.

The Simon & Schuster Speakers Bureau can bring authors
to your live event. For more information, or to book an event,
contact the Simon & Schuster Speakers Bureau at
1-866-248-3049 or visit our website at www.simonspeakers.com.

Manufactured in the United States of America

10 9 8 7 6 5 4 3 2

Library of Congress Cataloging-in-Publication Data is available.

ISBN 978-1-6680-2234-4
ISBN 978-1-6680-2236-8 (ebook)

For my sister, Lisa, who had to put up with me long before the rest of you.

CONTENTS

INTRODUCTION

I'm the humblest man I know.

No one is humbler than me. If there was an award for humbleness given out to the most deserving media member, I would have won it for eighteen straight years, ever since I sat down in front of the computer screen in my United States Virgin Islands law office—there are a ton of great stories to tell about those days—and began my media career in 2004.

I am the humblest man I know *even though* I have the best judgment on the planet. If King Solomon were alive today, his name would be Clay Travis. Most people are good at only a few things. I am, on the contrary, good at virtually everything. At least the things that really matter. Everything I am bad at doesn't matter. I asked my wife to give a list of things I am bad at, and here is what she provided: taking out the trash, disciplining our kids, cursing at the television screen when my teams are playing poorly, complaining about refereeing when coaching or watching our kids in sporting events, being patient, driving too fast, exaggerating all facts in my favor, refusing to wear undershirts (which means my nipples are too visible in white shirts), leaving newspapers lying around the house, not putting my clothes in the laundry, and managing to forget everything she tells me—as you can see, all inconsequential things. In particular I am good at solving problems. I believe that if you give me an intractable and unsolvable problem, I can solve it.

Every time.

Without fail.

Which is good because the biggest issue we have in our country right now is—everything is broken. This is because, to a large degree, our entire country has gone insane. That is why I am here with a book that, again, humbly, promises to solve every single issue facing America today.

If only people would just listen to me and do exactly what I say.

My goal with this book is simple: I want to make America sane again.

And solve every issue facing our country.

And I'm going to do it very humbly.

Chances are if you're reading this book, you are also fed up with the state of our country. You wonder how in the world we've reached a place where men are competing against women in sports—and even becoming women's champions! Where your kids had to wear worthless masks to school for years to protect them from a virus that posed them a statistical risk of zero, and if you even questioned whether that made sense you were an anti-science zealot. Where we decided to solve racism by capitalizing the *b* in Black and firing anyone who said All Lives Matter instead of Black Lives Matter.

How did we get here?

To a place where some of you—yes, I can see you—have pulled the dust jacket off this book so people won't know what you're reading at the pool. (And, come on, do you really think you can master all the arguments in this book if you're *drinking while reading it*? I mean, sure I was drunk when I wrote chapter four, but I'm the author and no one can see what I'm doing. You, you're in public, drinking and hiding the dust jacket of this book because you're afraid people might find out you like me. Your granddads and great-grandads were brave enough to storm the beaches of Normandy and you're too worried about what the mom showing way too much cleavage in her new bikini—tell my wife hi, by the way—is going to think about what you're reading at the pool. What a pathetic coward you are.)

Anyway, I'm here to save the country and lead us to an electoral landslide that will save us, once and for all, from the idiots who are currently leading our country.

I know most of you know me because I'm quite famous—and devilishly handsome, too, according to my mother, who has purchased ten thousand copies of this book and will have me personally sign them all for every person she will meet over the next five years—you think I'm joking, I'm not. But if you, perchance, are not aware of who I am, I'm a dad with three kids—that we know of—who went to college and law school before people became crazy, started writing about sports in my Caribbean law office in 2004, kept writing online even though a lot of people hoped I would die instead, started doing local sports talk radio in my hometown of Nashville, Tennessee, which led to national radio, and eventually founded a media company, Outkick, which I sold to Fox in 2021.

I am now very rich and don't have to work and have two beach houses in Florida because I couldn't decide which beach community I liked better. Also, my wife is gorgeous and a former NFL cheerleader for the Tennessee Titans, and she wants you to know that she hates the opening to this book and told me to change it because it makes me seem too cocky.

I grew up in Goodlettsville, Tennessee, a small suburb of Nashville, just on the edge of northern Davidson County, and if there are many typos and grammatical errors in this book it's because I went to public school from kindergarten to twelfth grade. Then I went to college at George Washington University. They gave me an academic scholarship, which is how I ended up there. GWU is the kind of school really rich kids go to when they aren't smart enough to get into Georgetown University, despite the fact that they've had every advantage in life. After GWU, I went to Vanderbilt Law School, where I met my wife. We met when I was recruiting good-looking girls for our intramural coed softball team. My wife can't field, hit, or throw, but she made the team and we have now been together for over twenty years. And now we have three sons, whom I am not allowed to name in this book because my wife wants them to be admitted to college one day. She says being connected to me makes that less likely.

I've been in media for nearly twenty years. As I said, I started with writing online from my Virgin Islands law office, and then that led to radio and TV. I now cohost the biggest radio show in the country—Buck Sexton and I took over for the late Rush Limbaugh in 2021—and have been doing daily television for both sports and politics, on Fox News, Fox, and FS1, for a long time now, too. One reason I've been successful is because of a major character flaw—I don't care what other people think of me. In fact, if ten people say something negative and one person says something positive, I remember the positive thing and forget, almost immediately, all the negatives.

In fact, even the people who hate me I think secretly like me.

I was out at a really fancy Los Angeles rooftop restaurant for the Super Bowl in 2021. It was one of those perfect LA days, not a cloud in the sky, the weather so perfect that the temperature indoors and outdoors was the exact same, and there were a ton of open tables. It was early afternoon, so I asked if there was a table available. The girl at the restaurant said there wasn't, so we went to the bar and stood there to have some drinks.

My companion, Alex Curry, then hosting a daily sports gambling show, *Fox Bet Live*, which was in its fourth year, said, "That girl totally hated you."

"Really? I didn't even notice."

And it's true, I didn't.

I'm still not sure she hated me. How could she? I'm amazing. But my point here isn't how amazing I am—we all already know that. It's that being concerned with what people you don't know think of you is a complete and total waste of time. I care what my wife and kids think of me. They live with me every single day. I care what people I work with think of me; they have to work with me. Those people know me. But why should I spend a single minute worried about what people I don't know think of me? And why should you care, either?

Several years ago I was out to dinner with former NBA superstar—and currently the best person on sports TV—Charles Barkley. Just so you know, I'm not the kind of guy who name-drops. I hate those people. Hold on, I have to stop writing now,

President Donald Trump just called me. Anyway, back to dinner with my good friend Charles. He said, "Clay, if you worry about the people who don't like you, then eventually the people who do like you won't like you anymore, either."

It's amazing advice and particularly true in our social media era, when people are judging you all day long for every possible issue. I'm convinced social media is the worst thing to happen to our country in my lifetime, but I'll get to that a bit later. In the meantime, you're probably thinking, Okay, Clay, I'm halfway through my drink and you still haven't told me how you're going to save the country.

That's a fair point. (Also, let's be honest, it's not your first drink. It's your third. And it's only ten in the morning. You should really pace yourself better; you might have a drinking problem.) But my editor has the same criticism. So let me tell you what I'm doing in this book. You may have noticed that we have an election coming up in 2024. It's kind of a big deal. The future of the free world hangs in the balance. And right now we have a doddering old man, Joe Biden, in charge of our country. After the 2022 election, which should have been a total seismic red tsunami but ended up being a red trickle instead, we've essentially had two straight 50–50 elections in this country. Which is why I want you to think about this for a minute. It's not just that Joe Biden is bad at being president, it's that Joe Biden is president and HE COULDN'T BE HIRED RIGHT NOW TO DO ANY OTHER JOB IN AMERICA. (Okay, maybe Walmart greeter.)

I'm not kidding about this. We've elected Joe Biden to the most important job in America and none of us would hire him to work at our businesses. There's not a single job Joe Biden could do at Outkick. Not one. He couldn't do any job at Fox News or any job at Fox Sports. He couldn't work on my radio show.

Hell, he couldn't host a single hour of my three-hour daily radio show.

You want him to fix gas prices?

Please.

Joe Biden couldn't run a single gas station anywhere in America.

So it's kind of a big deal that we've put a completely incompetent person in the most important job in the country. The first term of the Biden presidency has been like *Weekend at Bernie's*. Remember *Weekend at Bernie's*? It came out in 1989. The concept was two young guys show up at Bernie's house, only to find out he's dead. Then they pretend he isn't dead and hijinks ensue. The first movie was such a success they made *Weekend at Bernie's II*! Which will be the road map for Biden's reelection campaign in 2024.

This is the Biden presidency.

Only, unlike the *Weekend at Bernie's* movies, it's not successful.

At all.

Which is why I'm writing this book.

To stop this from ever happening again.

Now, you might be thinking, Why does a guy who used to talk about sports have any clue how to save the country from the idiots presently running it? Well, I actually think sports provide a good template for how to achieve success. In fact, is there anyone reading this right now who wouldn't rather have Alabama head football coach Nick Saban or New England Patriots head coach Bill Belichick as president right now instead of Joe Biden?

In fact, sometimes I think we've wasted Saban and Belichick on football. Sure, it's great they've won seven national titles and six Super Bowls between them, but football is just entertainment. Who wins the national title and the Super Bowl doesn't really change any of our lives.

I think Saban and Belichick would both probably be pretty good presidents because what we elect a president for is decision-making. They've both excelled at that for generations. But, again, what they do doesn't really matter that much in the larger context.

What if we have wasted these guys on sports? I mean, what if instead of becoming president, winning the Civil War, and ending slavery, Abraham Lincoln had ended up the head coach of Illinois basketball and won a bunch of national championships there? (I'm sorry for tantalizing you like this, Fighting Illini fans.) I mean, Illinois fans might be ecstatic, but wouldn't the rest of us be a bit concerned we'd wasted Lincoln's talents on something that didn't really matter?

Nick Saban and Bill Belichick are the exact opposite of Joe Biden. They would succeed at any job they had, from janitor to neurosurgeon. Biden is the complete opposite. He could only do one job, politician, and he sucks at it.

One of the biggest problems with our politics today is that we have way too many professional politicians. Joe Biden has been a politician for fifty years. Fifty years! That should never happen. The founding fathers never intended for someone to spend their entire life in politics. You shouldn't make a living in politics; you should make a living and then go into politics. Do your best for a decade or so in politics and then move on to something else.

The problem is that politics has become a profession. And

many people are afraid to say what they really believe because they're all terrified that if they do, they won't be able to get elected again. The reason I have a career at all is because I say exactly what I think, for better or worse.

My wife says the reason I have never needed therapy is because I have three hours of therapy every day on the radio. I say exactly what I think every day and all the weight is off my shoulders. Meanwhile, most of the rest of the country is terrified that if they say what they really think on Facebook, Instagram, Twitter, or whatever other social platform out there people use, they'll lose their job.

Put down your drinks for a minute there at the pool and raise your hand—yes, even you at the pool with the dust jacket off the book to hide what you're reading—if you've ever written something on social media that you really believe and then deleted it before you pressed post.

Boy, do you guys look ridiculous, raising your hand for no reason at the pool. Do you think I can see you? Stop drinking, I beg you.

A year ago at my speaking engagements—where I could actually see the people in the room—I started having everyone close their eyes and raise their hand if they'd ever deleted something before they posted it. The entire room would raise their hands. And I bet every single one of you reading this right now has also been afraid to say what you really think online at some point in the past several years. That's because we live in a terrified, censorious culture right now. All of us, Republicans, Democrats, and independents, know things are wrong in the country, but we don't have a plan to fix it.

Fully 75 percent of all voters said the country was on the wrong track in the 2022 elections. And then do you know what happened in the midterms? Every incumbent running for reelection in a statewide office but one got reelected. Think about this for a moment: the only senator or governor to lose his race in the entire country was Nevada governor Steve Sisolak.

How bad must that guy have sucked at his job?

And how in the world does this happen? How does everyone hate the direction the country is going and then reelect all the people who are making you hate how things are going in the country?! It makes me furious just writing this sentence.

Hell, Pennsylvania Democrats elected John Fetterman to the US Senate and he's nearly dead. Which sounds bad until you realize they ACTUALLY REELECTED A DEAD MAN TO THE PENNSYLVANIA STATEHOUSE. You think I'm joking, but I'm not. Tony DeLuca died in October 2022 and then won reelection after this death.

Can you imagine being the Republican who got beat by an actual dead man? Not the dead people who have been voting for Democrats for generations—I kid, I kid—but an actual dead man. Even for Democrats this is an impressive level of voting incompetence.

But it wasn't just Pennsylvania.

In every state that's going to be a toss-up in 2024—Wisconsin, Georgia, Nevada, Arizona, Pennsylvania, and New Hampshire—Republicans lost basically every statewide race that matters.

Plainly, this can't continue.

Well, I mean, it can, but the country will cease to exist, essentially. That's why I'm here writing a new book. Not because I need the money—I wrote the last three books because I needed the money, but now I'm rich—now I'm trying to save the country from all the idiots.

This book is a playbook to solve all the country's issues.

Those of you who played sports, especially football, remember the concept of a playbook. Your coach issues a playbook—at least if he's a decent coach—and you learn those plays so you can, hopefully, beat your opponent. But here's the deal: I don't just want to beat my opponent, I want to crush them. In fact, I don't believe that America can get back to sanity with a narrow victory; I want utter evisceration. I don't want to win 21–20 on a last-second touchdown; I want to win like Ronald Reagan did in 1984. I want a landslide in 2024.

And that's exactly what will happen if Republicans follow this playbook.

As you read, in addition to realizing how incredibly likable and handsome I am, you will also become aware of something else—I'm a huge history nerd. In fact, I'm such a history nerd that I have a proverbial trump card of historical nerd-dom—I actually went away to Civil War history camp.

Yep, after my junior year of high school I traveled to Gettysburg College for Civil War sleepaway camp. I was a scholarship kid at the camp thanks to the excellent essay I wrote that netted me the free ride—when she heard about this my wife said, "People competed for that?!"—and I am still a huge history nerd. In fact, if the multiverse exists there is probably a college history professor version of Clay Travis out there somewhere. (There's probably also a few versions where I'm in prison, too, so let's not get too excited about the multiverse.)

I've been a history nerd my entire life. In fact, my very first idol was none other than Davy Crockett, whose most famous life motto, one that I've adopted for my life as well, was "Be sure you're right and then go ahead."

Well, I'm sure I'm right, so let's go ahead.

CHAPTER I

WHEN YOU'RE LOSING, CHANGE THE PLAYBOOK

When you are losing just about every game, your first goal is this: stop getting your ass kicked. And the way you stop getting your ass kicked is by first acknowledging everything that you've been doing is wrong. For much of the past thirty years Republicans have been the huge losers. You can't win until you acknowledge that you're losing, and that's what Republicans have been doing, pretty much, since 1992.

My playbook is designed to end the ass kickings. There are many issues that Republicans are concerned about—tax policy, the national debt, things that I have strong opinions on, too— but they aren't landslide issues, issues that 60 percent or more of the American public will agree with going forward. What I'm focused on in this book is creating a landslide. I don't want to win in 2024 by a proverbial last-second field goal. I want a complete and total evisceration, a rout, a beatdown that leaves Democrats crying in the corner clutching their Dr. Anthony Fauci pillows. But before you can win, you have to eliminate the ass kickings. The Republican program is not, right now, a successful team. It's Alabama before Nick Saban arrived, the New England Patriots before Bill Belichick (and Tom Brady). It's a freaking dumpster fire of presidential election incompetence. Hell, we just lost to Joe Fucking Biden . . . and now Democrats are so cocky they are going to run Joe Biden again, planning on a presidential sequel election, *Weekend at Bernie's II*!

Since 1992 the Democratic Party has won seven of the eight presidential elections in the popular vote. The only Republican to win the popular vote and the presidency in the past thirty years was George W. Bush in 2004.

In more than two hundred years of American presidential politics no political party has had a stretch of dominance that has run for this long. Whatever you think of Donald Trump's presidency—I happen to think it was pretty fantastic—he lost the popular vote in 2016 and in 2020. He won a very close race in 2016 and lost a very close election in 2020. If Trump is the nominee in 2024, it is likely that the election will again come down to a tiny difference.

I'm not going to spend a ton of time in this book discussing the 2020 election because the 2022 midterm election showed us that whatever you think about the 2020 election's outcome, just about every major candidate who spent substantial time talking about 2020 lost in the 2022 midterms. In battleground states like Pennsylvania, Georgia, Nevada, and Arizona, places that Republicans absolutely, positively have to win in 2024, all the candidates who focused most aggressively on the 2020 election being stolen lost. That's because independent voters—and also many Republican voters in these states—overwhelmingly reject the idea that the 2020 election was stolen, and even Republican voters won't support people who deny the 2020 election results. In 2022, Kari Lake, who I think was an absolutely phenomenal candidate, lost the Arizona governor's race by 17,000 votes. Katie Hobbs, who is a joke of a candidate, even for a Democrat, got 50.3 percent of the vote and Kari Lake got 49.7 percent. That loss—and I know, I know, there are always arguments that elections are stolen, trust me, I get all your emails and Facebook messages, but the courts have rejected those claims in 2020 and in 2022—featured independents turning against Lake, but many Republicans didn't vote for her, either. Lake got 40,000 fewer Republican votes than down-ballot Republican candidates did in Maricopa County, where the majority of Arizonans live. While people can fume about Democrats and independent voters, if Republicans had voted for Lake, she would have won comfortably. Indeed, the overall turnout of voters was Republican +9 in Arizona—PLUS NINE—yet both Lake and Senate candidate Blake Masters lost their statewide races.

And it wasn't just in Arizona.

Despite the fact that I am a University of Tennessee football fan, I campaigned heavily for former University of Georgia running back Herschel Walker in his Senate run in Georgia. Herschel narrowly lost on November 8, 2022, and then narrowly lost again in the runoff in December. (Georgia requires runoffs when neither statewide candidate for office receives over 50 percent of the vote.) Significantly, Walker lost despite the fact that every other Republican running for statewide office in Georgia, the other seven Republicans, won comfortably, including Georgia governor Brian Kemp, who smoked Stacey Abrams by nearly eight full points.

The numbers on election night were stark. Kemp beat Abrams 2,111,572 to 1,813,673 in the Georgia governor's race, a margin of 297,899. Compare that with Walker, who lost to Democrat Raphael Warnock, 1,946,117 to 1,908,442, on election night, a margin of 37,675 in favor of Warnock. That margin increased to nearly 100,000 for Warnock in the runoff. That's because voters, many of them Republicans, split their tickets for Georgia governor and US Senate races. Walker got roughly 200,000 fewer votes on election night in 2022 than Kemp and the rest of the Republicans on the statewide ticket did.

Now, Walker was, I believe, unfairly attacked throughout the 2022 race for past issues, but he was also directly connected to Trump's allegations of 2020 election fraud, which also cost Republicans two Senate seats in 2020. (Democrats won both Georgia US Senate seats in runoff elections in 2020.) Walker didn't lose, however, because of Democrats; he lost because Republicans didn't support him the same way they supported the other seven statewide candidates in 2022.

You can argue that Warnock was simply a good candidate and that's why Walker lost. But the numbers don't bear that out. Warnock won with substantially less voting support in 2022 than he received in 2020. Warnock was ripe to be beaten. Republicans just didn't manage to do it. Because Republicans split their tickets. The Georgia US Senate race, in my opinion, wasn't won by Democrats, it was lost by Republicans.

You may still be furious about 2020—heck, I'm still furious about 2020, too, because the result has been Joe Biden's disastrous tenure—but the data on independent voters and many Republicans reflects that they don't want to look back. They want a vision for the future. So if Donald Trump is the nominee in 2024 and he focuses backward on 2020, he's going to lose.

Period.

I don't want to lose, which is why I'm going to be sure Trump and his team, along with every other Republican running for president, get early copies of this book!

This book is a game plan for winning a substantial majority in 2024. If the Republican nominee adopts my suggestions, he or she will win comfortably. If they don't, I think they'll lose.

Again.

And Democrats will have won the popular vote for eight of the past nine elections.

Full disclosure: I don't want this book to be overwhelmed by Donald Trump and his politics. I voted for Trump in 2020. He should have won that election because Joe Biden was an awful candidate with bad policy ideas. The past several years have proven that Biden is a disaster, the worst president in any of our lives. But just pointing out how bad Biden has been isn't enough. That was the game plan in 2022 and it didn't work to win the Senate and it barely won the House. We need to provide an argument about what we will do that's better than what Biden has done.

This probably won't surprise you, but I humbly believe that if we could go back in time and I could be inside Donald Trump's body for the 2020 presidential debates against Joe Biden and answer every question for him, Trump would have won comfortably in 2020. I really do. Especially in the first debate against Biden, Trump was the worst advocate possible for all of his policies.

But the reason I'm writing a book to guarantee a landslide is to eliminate the funny business, the fickle hand of fate that can swing elections one way or the other based on how many floods hit Atlanta precincts while they're still counting ballots.

I don't want 2024 to be close.

I want to go to bed on election night in 2024, probably drunk, without having to worry about absentee ballots in Wisconsin or to wait for weeklong tallies in Pennsylvania, Georgia, Arizona, and Nevada. I want Rachel Maddow, Don Lemon, and Joy Reid to be crying live on-air by 11 p.m. eastern.

I want a landslide because if you lose a close election—or a close game—you convince yourself you could have won if only you'd just executed a bit better.

But do you know what happens when you get your ass kicked?

You don't blame the play calling or the officiating or a single play for your loss. You recognize that your playbook is fundamentally flawed. And let's be clear, the Democrat playbook is broken. They are running the Wing T in an era of the spread offense. (For those of you who aren't football zealots, the Wing T was a football offense that existed before passing overtook football. That's the Democrat playbook; it's antediluvian.) But Republicans haven't taken advantage of this.

Nor have they won a transformative electoral victory that ends all the suspense.

At least not yet.

That's because the Republican playbook has been even worse than the Democrat playbook for most of the twenty-first century. We don't run good plays, and even when we do, we turn the ball over and let Democrats run out the clock.

Hell, Joe Biden won in 2020 barely leaving his basement.

But it's not just Republican ineptitude. For most of this century neither party has really been able to win a massive, transformative victory.

Think about it. Every presidential race in the twenty-first century, with the exception of one—Barack Obama's triumph over John McCain in 2008—has left every American, whether Democrat, Republican, or independent, convinced their side could have won if only some small issue had been altered. Squint your eyes tightly enough and Al Gore wins in 2000—heck, maybe Gore really did win in 2000—John Kerry triumphs in 2004, Mitt Romney is president in 2012, Hillary Clinton in 2016, and Donald Trump, I know, I know, wins reelection in 2020. All of these outcomes are eminently reasonable potential results of our elections if only a tiny difference in electoral math had occurred.

Yes, they didn't happen, but they could have happened with a subtle alteration of the electoral math. If it sometimes feels to you as if we've fine-tuned our election to such an extent that we might as well walk up to the front porch of a midsize home in Scranton, Pennsylvania, and ask the fifty-six-year-old husband and wife living in that house to tell us whether they are voting for the Democrat or Republican candidate for president this year, you're not that far from the truth.

There simply aren't very many swing voters in swing states.

Change just 20,000 votes in Wisconsin, Arizona, and Georgia

out of the 156 million cast for president in 2020 and Donald Trump and Joe Biden would have tied 269–269 in the electoral count, tossing the election to the House of Representatives, where Trump would have won the election after the state congressional members broke the tie in his favor. And if you think Democrats wouldn't have stormed the Capitol and fomented their own "insurrection" if that tiebreak scenario happened, you didn't pay attention to the entirety of the 2020 "mostly peaceful" protests for "social justice."

Remember, they didn't board up cities all over America because they were worried Biden would win; they boarded up all American cities in case Trump won reelection. Democrats would have 100 percent stormed the Capitol, in my opinion, if Trump had flipped 20,000 more votes in Wisconsin, Arizona, and Georgia and won a tiebreaker in the Electoral College in the House of Representatives.

My point is that each party is committed to an ironclad electoral strategy that leaves us all bleary-eyed the night after an election because we stayed up all night to see what a couple of people in Scranton decided to do with their presidential vote. That's how fine-tuned the electoral calculus has become. Each side, essentially, is committed to an election plan that offers the narrowest possible path to victory. And when defeat comes, that defeat isn't, generally speaking, accepted with magnanimity, it's immediately believed to be rooted in cheating. The same Democrats lecturing us today about Republicans threatening the sanctity of our democracy with their 2020 election denials spent four years saying Trump's 2016 election was the product of Russian collusion and conspiracy.

The only way to change this paradigm is with an electoral victory that's seismic in nature, one that both sides have to accept, a victory so substantial that no shenanigans can alter the outcome.

This is why coming to politics from the world of sports is helpful.

I've seen all of this before. Frankly, it's what happens in any sporting event that comes down to the final couple of plays when an official is forced to make a controversial call that determines the outcome of a game. Our political elections come down to field goal kicks, and those field goal opportunities often come down to whether an official does or does not call pass interference on the final drive of the game.

Every presidential election is the 2019 NFC Championship Game between the Los Angeles Rams and New Orleans Saints—sorry, Saints fans—all over again. One call makes the difference because the margin is so tight. (I'm still bitter over this outcome because I lost, and I'm ashamed to admit this, $30,000 betting alongside my friend cousin Sal for the Saints to win this game. Yes, *thirty thousand dollars because an official blew a readily apparent pass-interference call that anyone with functional eyesight clearly saw.* Forgive me, this one still stings.)

It's Super Bowl LVII, where every Philadelphia Eagles fan reading this right now is screaming that the final holding penalty on their defensive back—which allowed the Kansas City Chiefs to run out the clock and kick a field goal—was wrongly made. Every Cincinnati Bengals fan is also screaming that they were screwed in the AFC Championship Game.

My point: no one argues about officiating calls in blowouts!

So how do you break this election cycle of close wins and close losses and end all the complaining about rigged elections? It requires taking a risk, and following a game plan that might look risky in the short term but is brilliant in the long term. You have to disrupt the existing political calculus, and you have to do it in a way where the vast majority of the voters are being served. And I believe it's actually not that difficult to do.

It just requires bravery and clarity of purpose.

In fact, Donald Trump started to do it, but he didn't do it enough; Trump wasn't enough of a disrupter to actually create a landslide victory for Republicans. To be fair, he might have won a landslide in 2020 without Covid, which I'll discuss later, but Covid was the wild card that made 2020 winnable for Democrats. Otherwise, I believe, Trump would have won reelection based on a great economy. But even Trump, who remade the Republican Party with his win in 2016, didn't go far enough to create a lasting political legacy. It takes blowout wins to change the country for generations.

In theory, either political party could commit to winning a landslide victory, but everyone is so afraid of losing the voters they already have that they aren't willing to take a risk to gain far more voters than they have today. And why would Democrats change considering they've won seven of the last eight elections? The disruptive party is almost always the loser, the team that hasn't executed a win yet.

It's not a coincidence that most football ingenuity comes from the upstarts, the challengers, the underdogs. The teams that have been losing develop a new style of offense or defense. The incumbent powers evolve the slowest, which is why the biggest American businesses eventually become obsolete.

The fear of change is commonplace in all facets of life. It's called risk aversion. Most people fear losing what they already have more than they crave attaining more. I might have a screw loose in my head, but I've worked to try to eliminate fear from my life. I was an incredibly fearful kid. I could never fall asleep at night because I was always convinced people were going to break into our house and murder us. I spent years expecting to be murdered, every night. The fact that my bedroom was the first one you passed in our family's hallway meant I was doomed to die first. No one would hear me scream.

Overcome with terror in the middle of the night, I would leap out of bed and sprint into my parents' bedroom, where I would climb up between the two of them. I did this for years, until I was twelve years old. My parents even started joking with me about how often I jumped into their bed, asking where we were all going to go on our honeymoon when I got married. Sometimes—and this is even funnier now that I have kids of my own—I even used to crawl in bed with other people's parents when I got scared sleeping over at friends' houses. (Some of those other people's parents are even reading this book right now—hi, Pam; hi, Tim; hi, Susan! Yes, I really grew up and now do TV and radio and write books. America's amazing!)

Overcoming risk aversion in my own life was an incredible battle. And it didn't end when I hit adulthood. I was in my twenties when I really, seriously conquered fear in my own life and started to become comfortable analyzing risk and taking chances.

But once I did, I saw opportunity everywhere. Conquering fear in my own life helped me see how much fear there was everywhere and how many people, even successful ones, were totally paralyzed by fear. Indeed, sometimes success is a great paralyzer. Because once you have some measure of success, it can make you even more risk-averse than before. When you don't have much, it's easier to take risks because you don't have a lot to lose. But what about once you have a house and a good job? Then taking that next risky step can be virtually impossible. Young lawyers experience this early in our careers. We even have a name for it: the golden handcuffs. Yes, you're making good money, often for the first time in your life—aka the golden handcuffs, but that good money can keep you from taking the risks that you otherwise would to find a more fulfilling career. It's why every lawyer in the country, including all of you reading this right now, has a fantasy job, one they would actually prefer to be doing if they could.

That's why back in the fall of 2006 I left the full-time practice of law to write a book about traveling around to every Southeastern Conference (SEC) football stadium.

Do you know how many people have ever made that career change, going from practicing law to writing a book about a college football road trip?

Zero.

Literally I am the only one.

If I'd been worried about what other people thought or had been worried about losing what I already had, I would have never taken this risk. But I wasn't excited about practicing law and I was excited about writing the book on Southeastern Conference football. (The book is still out there, *Dixieland Delight*, and it's still a fun read; you should check it out if you haven't already.)

So I wrote the book and now I'm a hundred-millionaire. (Again, I say humbly.)

I would have never taken this risk if I feared failure. And guess what? What if I had failed? What if I'd been wrong about being able to make a living in sports media and gone back to practicing law? At least I would have taken the chance. Once I had the law degree, "failure" just meant I'd keep doing what I was already doing. There actually wasn't very much risk at all.

If you're reading this book right now and you're not doing something because you're afraid you're going to fail—especially if you're young and don't have kids—what in the world are you afraid of? Don't be a pussy, #dbap, go for it.

I'll give you another quick story that makes this point as well. When I first started working on sports radio in Nashville, our local sports station was successful. But it wasn't as successful, in my mind, as it could be.

But no one wanted to rock the boat. They didn't really want to risk losing the audience that we already had. The overall mindset was to just avoid making a mistake and leave well enough alone. We were constantly warned about how losing listeners for any reason would lead to our ratings tanking. (Advertising rates are based on the number of listeners you have, so losing listeners would be destructive to the business of sports talk radio.) That fear of failure stifled creativity in my mind and, even worse than that, it created really boring programming.

Early in my sports radio tenure, in the summer of 2009 legendary Green Bay Packers quarterback Brett Favre came out of retirement and decided he was going to play for the Minnesota Vikings. This was a huge story in sports, as you can well imagine and may recall. Soon after this return, Favre was accused, unfortunately, of sending unsolicited penis pics to a female employee of the New York Jets, where Favre had played for one season in 2008. Right after that story broke, Favre, an aging quarterback at this point, did a press conference where he talked about how many different body parts he had that were hurting.

But he tried to avoid addressing the penis pics allegation, even as he discussed the health of his other body parts in great detail.

We played the live audio of that Favre press conference, and then I had our radio producer stop every few seconds and instead of talking about his injured body part, I would talk about how Favre's penis felt instead of whatever body part he was addressing. I probably did it for a couple of minutes. The point was to satirize that while everyone was talking about the penis pics scandal, Favre was talking about every other body part.

As sports talk radio bits go, it was pretty funny. The great thing about live radio, in general, is that it isn't planned. It's live. There's no script. You just have to trust your instincts about what makes good radio. Joking about Brett Favre's penis during an otherwise boring radio press conference was, in my opinion, good radio.

But complaints immediately flooded into the radio station because I'd said the word *penis* too many times. Our phone lines were on fire and everyone wanted to weigh in with an opinion. Some people in this scenario would run from controversy, but I know good radio and knew that taking angry calls about my use of the word *penis* was radio gold. (I've always said the number one test for good radio is whether someone will stay in their car when they reach their destination. If you've been at work all day and you pull into your garage and don't want to leave the car because you want to know what's going to happen next? That's *great* radio. I still believe the best radio segment I've ever done was when we had two girls who got in a catfight at a Nashville horse race call in, and I interviewed them like it was *60 Minutes*. I should have gotten a Pulitzer for that interview. Most of you right now are thinking, I'd like to hear that interview. Of course you would. Because it was *great* radio.)

Anyway, some callers were furious that I would use the word *penis* on the radio, but almost all of them were using the word *penis* in their calls to complain about me using the word *penis*. Eventually an older man with an impeccable southern accent called in to question my use of the word *penis* on the radio because his wife was in the car with him and she had been scandalized by my behavior.

I told this gentleman that I respected his opinion and wanted to ensure that I would never use a word that would offend him on the radio again. I told him I had a list of words for body parts in front of me and would go through them one by one to decide what the appropriate line for radio behavior was. (I didn't actually have a list, but I'm pretty good on the fly.)

So I started with the word *bottom*.

"Sir," I said, "what if I used the word *bottom* on the radio. Would that be okay?"

There was a long pause.

Finally our southern gentleman responded in his long drawl, "That would be borderline."

And just like that, to the extent anyone had disagreed with me, I had them all back on my side. Because no one could really say the word *bottom* was unacceptable to say on the radio in 2009. Whatever the standard was for acceptable vocabulary, this caller had missed his mark.

I always liked taking calls on sports radio because most of the people who were upset about something I had said would tell on themselves if you let them talk with you long enough on the radio. That's because the overwhelming majority of people in the country are reasonable. And, significantly, they also recognize reasonableness when they hear it. Just about everyone, as we'll discuss in a bit, hates cancel culture, and when you actually force the people who want to cancel things to make their case these people generally lose the argument.

But the old man's call didn't mean the story was over.

Back in 2009, we had a new people meter in the market—this meter measured actual listener behavior as opposed to doing ratings based on a paper diary, which was the old way of tallying listeners. The number of people who had these people meters was tiny, so only a few people in each market would determine what the entire city's radio ratings were. It turned out that with an actual meter on, people listened to classical music way less than they claimed in a paper diary. Who knew?

Our boss, whom I loved working for, emailed me after the penis radio incident.

And I swear to God, this is the actual email I received on Wednesday, August 10, 2009. I still have it in my inbox.

The subject line:

Penis feedback

And this was the entire email:

You know how I feel about it. It's not overtly offensive, but you've got to understand the total audience.

I was just in a meeting that showed me that on average, 5 listeners represent your entire audience. 5 TOTAL PEOPLE.

If those 5 people are put off, you lose your entire audience.

In a month, I'm going to show you what it did to your listening audience.

Here's what I'm getting . . .

I know you have been bombarded with comments about the Three Hour Lunch program but I would be regretful if I too didn't comment. The continuous use of "Penis" was childish but not the real issue. The real issue is the disrespect to listeners who were bold enough to complain, especially the 70 year old man. Mrs. Grissoms can't be happy. Always been a proud listener of the shows but today I lost some respect for The Zone.

YOUR ENDLESS PENIS COMMENTS WILL COST YOU MANY MANY LISTENERS YOU WILL BEFIRED! [*sic*]

You have lost a 3 hour lunch listener. I know penis is not a foul word but I don't want to hear it repeated several times during the Brent [*sic*] Farve [*sic*] press conference with my young kids in the car with me. It was rude of the 3 hour lunch crew to talk over the press confrence [*sic*] and say what they did during it.

I quote "how my penis feels good" who wants to hear that on the radio.

These were representative samples of the deluge of emails my boss was getting. If you think these are bad, you should have seen what happened when I went on local Birmingham radio back in 2007 and suggested the University of Alabama should replace fired football coach Mike Shula with the disinterred remains of

Bear Bryant, the only person who could satisfy the Alabama faithful. (I really did this. My buddy Lance Taylor, still doing shows in Alabama, says people still talk about this. The joke ended up being on me, however, because Alabama hired Nick Saban and my Tennessee Vols went on to lose for fifteen straight years to him until last year's glorious win in Knoxville.)

I responded to my boss's email about the anger over my use of the word *penis* by guaranteeing that our audience would go up and asking a question: Why do we only talk about losing the audience we already have? Why don't we spend more time talking about getting an audience we don't already have?

Now, this was in 2009, early in my radio career, but what do you think happened? Our radio show ratings skyrocketed. Everyone was talking about our segment and the penis controversy. We couldn't have bought the free advertising. And the people who claimed they were offended? They were the most likely to keep listening, because they wanted to know what I might say next.

To his credit, my boss at the station, Brad Willis, who had hired me and was a big fan of my content, never complained about any other segment I ever did in local radio once he got the ratings data back. He understood good radio and he saw that we were expanding the audience in ways that we never had before.

He'd just been doing what most people do in business, politics, or sports—when you have success, protect it. Don't risk the dollar that's already in your pocket.

Now, I was young at this point in my radio career and didn't have many dollars in my pocket, but one lesson I've learned in media, and already suspected back then, is this: as long as you aren't facing jail time, all publicity is good publicity. (And Donald

Trump might even prove this wrong with the charges being brought against him.)

It's difficult to cut through the daily noise and make people care about your opinion on anything. Having people talking about something they heard, read, or saw, whether good or bad, is the best free advertising that exists anywhere.

I've never set out to intentionally create controversy, but honesty is so rare that if you truly say what you think every single day, people seek you out.

By the next year we had the highest ratings for a sports talk radio show anywhere in the country. Our audience surged to levels it had never attained before, to levels our bosses didn't even think were possible. Why? Because if you're trying to protect what you've already got, you're going to lose. You have to always be advancing, never retreating.

Otherwise you will never grow.

If you are making arguments about 2020, you aren't advancing, you're fighting a rearguard action. Elections are about the future. You don't win by continuing to fight a race you already lost. That game's over.

Forever.

Which brings us back to my election strategy. There's too much fear in politics. It reminds me of my early radio career: success breeds inertia. Everyone is afraid of losing the voters they do have. That's loser thinking.

Sure, you may lose some voters by changing your strategy, but guess what? You will gain far more than you lose. And most of the people who claim they're leaving? They stay with you, too. Where else are they going to go?

But the best part of it all is, you end up with a better product.

Our radio show was better after the fear was gone. When you give people the freedom to take risks, you benefit. I think the same lesson of me saying "penis" on the radio can apply to politics, too. In fact, it applies even better.

I was already at a successful radio station, so the fear there was that they would blow up something that worked; they were already winning, I was just trying to get them to win bigger. But, let's be honest, Republicans have lost seven of the last eight national elections when it comes to the popular vote. What in the world are you afraid of? You're already losing elections. You're the group that should be challenging the existing paradigm, disrupting the existing game plan, trying something new. The Democrats are locked in. The team that's winning never changes strategy. They just keep running the same plays until one day they get their ass kicked by the insurgency.

Which brings me to a lesson I've learned about politics in a relatively short period of time. Most politicians are incredibly fearful people. They're terrified of losing an election so badly that they hope no one notices them while they're in office.

I just don't get this at all.

Again, maybe I'm just a weird unicorn here, but if I lost a political election, do you know how much different my life would be from what it was before?

There would be zero difference!

I'd still have a pretty good life. As I wrote earlier, I'm not doing these jobs because I have to do them. I'm doing them because I enjoy them and think I can make a difference in a positive way in this country.

I tell my wife all the time that at some point I'm going to take my phone and throw it as far as I can into the ocean and be unreachable.

She doesn't think I'll ever do it.

But if I could make the country sane again, I'd step out of the political arena in a heartbeat and go back to doing sports full-time. Hell, I'd retire and just travel the world and you guys would never hear from me again. But I keep looking around waiting for people to say the things I'm saying and almost no one is saying them. Every now and then I wonder if I'm the crazy person.

I just don't see how anything I'm saying is remotely controversial.

I think it's all just basic, common sense.

One of the real problems we have in this country is we have a ton of politicians who literally could do no other job except for being a politician. I mean, think about it for a minute. There is not one job at our Outkick website that Joe Biden could do.

As a bare minimum, shouldn't we require success in some part of life other than politics before we get people involved in politics? If you haven't succeeded in anything in life, why do I want you making decisions for the country?

There needs to be less fear of failure in politics. Yes, you could run for elective office and lose. That's a consequence of every election, just like there's a consequence of every sporting event: one person wins and the other loses.

But so what?

Losing isn't the worst thing that can happen to you. The worst thing that can happen to you is to be so afraid of losing that you take no risks. Trust me, I know—I used to run and jump into bed with my parents because I was convinced I was going to get murdered every night while I was sleeping.

And it was no way to live!

Especially not for my parents.

Side note one: I totally thought all my kids would be terrified to sleep by themselves, too, but none of them had any issues with sleep at all.

Side note two: Not only was I terrified that I would get murdered while sleeping, but I also was a big sleepwalker. In fact, to this day I regularly get out of bed and sleepwalk. I'll even open doors and run outside sometimes, convinced that someone is chasing me.

Just the other day I ran outside my house, just in my boxer shorts, and woke up only because it was so cold outside. Once, in law school, I slept-ran outside into the parking lot, where I crouched behind my car because I was convinced someone was chasing me.

It was the middle of the night and for some reason the maintenance guy was out walking around, too. It would have been really funny if he'd been sleepwalking, too, but instead he just said, "You okay, man?"

And I just sort of nodded and walked back to my apartment, nearly naked, shivering in the Nashville night.

I also have regular nightmares that there are snakes in our bed. I'm not sure anyone hates snakes more than me. I'm a total snakist. On the old radio show we used to debate whether there was any woman hot enough to date who had snakes as pets. My answer was no. If a woman has a pet snake, I'm turning around and walking right out of the house.

To this day, my wife will regularly roll over and say, when she sees me sprinting out of our bed and yelling uproariously in fear, "There are no snakes in the bed, Clay. You are sleepwalking."

Imagine how used to me she is if in the middle of the night I scream out there are snakes in the bed and she's totally calm and telling me we'll all be fine.

But also, what happens if one day there really are snakes in the bed?!

It's a total boy-who-cried-wolf scenario.

My sleep issues notwithstanding, I'm here to win landslide elections.

And Republicans are the only party that can win by a landslide in 2024 because Democrats aren't willing to take any real risks. Democrats have won seven of the last eight elections. They just sit back and run the same game plan: call Republicans racist and run up the votes.

Democrats are so cocky now it feels like they just trot out crazy-ass things to say to see what they can get away with. I mean, good Lord, Democrats are actually arguing that men can get pregnant now. Why are they making that argument? Because they are terrified of the transgender community turning on them. Their identity-politics-focused party is unable to disrupt their election calculus. Plus, let's be honest, it's fair for Democrats to argue that they don't need to change anything. After all, they're the ones who are winning.

But just as Bill Clinton looked around in 1992 and realized that a new Democratic Party had to ascend (remember, at that point Democrats had lost the popular vote in 1968, 1972, 1980, 1984, and 1988—their only win was Jimmy Carter in the

Watergate-fueled 1976 election) Republicans now need to embrace a new party platform. Republicans, increasingly, are becoming the party of sanity. But in order to win a landslide election, a Ronald Reagan–like destruction of their opponents, the modern-day Republican Party tent has to become even broader than it is today.

The Democrats are still winning, but they have a gargantuan branding problem. Namely, most Americans of all races hate woke politics. Which is why the moment is ripe for a Republican breakthrough. So how do Republicans brand themselves in a way that helps win an election landslide in 2024?

CHAPTER 2

WHAT'S YOUR TEAM IDENTITY?

Every playbook requires an offensive philosophy, something you specialize in doing, the plays you run that, if executed correctly, will lead to victory on the field. Some playbooks focus on running, others focus on passing. The best offensive philosophy, however, requires a mix of passing and running because it makes the offense unpredictable for the defense.

No two playbooks are the exact same, but every team has one, and regardless of the offensive philosophy, every team has to first decide what the essence of their team is. Are they physical or fast, explosive or plodding, consistent or unpredictable? That's what the playbook is, a story of success that's being shared, a plan to win.

But before we can execute our playbook, we have to first decide, what's the Republican story? What's the method that will lead to a 2024 landslide?

Well, fortunately, and as always, humbly, you have the perfect coach.

In addition to getting a law degree at Vanderbilt, I also got a master of fine arts degree in creative writing at Vanderbilt. (The Vanderbilt English Department is going to probably rescind that MFA the moment this book is published and becomes an immediate bestseller.)

It won't surprise you, but I thought I was an incredible creative writing teacher at Vanderbilt. In fact, if I hadn't ended up doing radio and TV and dominating all facets of media due to my incredible wealth of talent, there's an alternate universe where I would have ended up living in a quiet college town, spending no time on the Internet, never doing radio or TV, and just writing books and teaching college kids writing.

Let's pause for a moment and think about how much America would have lost out if I'd taken that career path instead. Boy, are you all lucky to have me?!

During my creative writing professorship back in 2006, I taught the college kids a lesson I believe is incredibly important: all stories, no matter how great or consequential, can be boiled down to a single sentence. I took this lesson partly from the world of creative writing, but also from the legal profession, where every case is boiled down to a question of the case. On some level, every legal dispute can be reduced to a question that a jury or a judge must decide.

The most famous court case of the past fifty years is probably the O. J. Simpson murder trial. The issue for the jury in Los Angeles in 1995 was quite simple: Did O. J. Simpson murder Nicole Brown Simpson and Ronald Goldman? There were other questions, to be sure, but the case boiled down to that simple question:

Did O.J. commit double murder or not? (Of course he did, but you see the point of this exercise.)

I'm a big believer in distilling complex concepts down to their essence, because that's how you talk to the largest possible audience. I've been talking to large audiences of people for a long time now. If you're reading this book and you listen to my radio show, you can probably hear my voice in your head as your read these sentences. That's intentional. Many years ago I decided I wanted my columns, my radio show, and my TV appearances to have a common voice. I didn't want to sound different on different platforms.

I wanted to write like I talk, and vice versa.

The challenge of writing for radio and TV is you're speaking to large audiences on a daily basis and those audiences all bring different skill sets to your analysis. So you have to be capable of speaking to a neurosurgeon and a janitor at the same time, and have both of these people understand and appreciate what you're saying. Then you add in age differences, too. You might be talking to an eighteen-year-old and an eighty-year-old. How can you connect with all these people with all these different backgrounds? And that's when it hit me early in my career—you have to do what a trial lawyer does: speak to the entire jury in a compelling way. Whether they are a grandmother or a teenage boy, you have to connect with everyone.

The way you do it is through story, even in sports, because, honestly, a play in a playbook is really just a written story of how a particular football play should go if it's executed properly. And, by the way, what's a play designed to do? Score a touchdown on offense or prevent one on defense, right? At its most basic level, football is a game of space. Offensive plays are designed to create space and defensive plays are designed to eliminate space. That's the entire point of every play for both the offense and the defense: the offense is trying to put a player where everyone isn't, and the defense is trying to put a player where everyone is. Football is a violent mirror.

In a jury trial the lawyer who tells the best story wins. The same thing is true in elections. Every election, at its most basic level, is just a storytelling contest, and the person who tells the best one wins. So what's the story that Republicans need to tell in 2024 to win an election?

Well, that feels a bit challenging, right? This is, after all, what political consultants get paid hundreds of millions of dollars to come up with. It can feel overwhelming to synthesize an entire political campaign down to one sentence. So, to demystify this process, let's start by practicing on television shows and popular movies, which may feel less overwhelming.

See, I'm a big believer that the best movies speak to everyone of all ages. The Pixar films nail this perfectly—whether you're six years old or eighty years old, you can watch a Pixar movie and get something out of it. (For purposes of this lesson we're pretending *Lightyear* doesn't exist, and that it's several years ago, before Disney went fully woke and decided every character in their films needed lesbian parents and a transgender brother/sister.) How do they do this? Well, there are many tricks—you put characters of different ages in the films. For instance in *Up* you have the grandfatherly hero, but you also have the kid Russell—but ultimately the films have to be constructed in such a way that their themes are timeless and universal. And their story in a sentence has to be flawlessly constructed.

Let me take you through exactly what I mean here.

If you're old enough to remember *TV Guide*—a print magazine that told you what was going to be on TV that week—every episode came with a tease. That was the story in a sentence for the TV programs airing that week. You could scan the sentence and almost immediately know whether the show was a new one or a rerun.

Back in the day when *Friends* aired, the story in a sentence might be: "Ross and Rachel's relationship hits a snag when it's discovered that Ross slept with someone else during their relationship break."

As a way to learn how to craft compelling stories, I used to teach the kids in my creative writing class to sum up the stories they were writing for our class in a sentence. I would also have them do this for every short story we read all year in class. The better you can simplify a story, the less mysticism there is when it comes to writing and the more you understand the story being told.

One of the biggest challenges young writers face is simply having the confidence to sit down in front of a blank screen and start writing. That's why I always tell young kids who want to be writers to walk to the area in a bookstore where their book would be. If you want to write a nonfiction history book, go there. If you want to write a work of fiction, head there.

Then go to the books and walk to the area where your last name is.

Maybe there's someone with the same last name as you, but probably there isn't.

Regardless, boom, that's where your book would go.

I used to do this all the time when I was a kid. I'd walk to the section of the bookstore, find the T's, and go stand directly in front of the section where a book written by Clay Travis would go. I didn't know any writers, I didn't know any publishers, I didn't know the first thing about writing a book. But starting at about the age of eight or nine years old, I'd go stand in front of the T's in the book section and visualize that one day I'd have a book there.

And now I do.

That's because the first obstacle to any person who wants to do anything is their own mind. You have to convince yourself it's possible. Once you do that, it is.

For decades no runner could break a four-minute mile.

Then Roger Bannister did it in 1954.

Within a few years, dozens of others had done it. Why? Because they knew it was possible. Belief in yourself is the most important single asset any person can have in this world. And in order to believe in yourself, you have to see it in your own mind before anyone else can, because no one else can convince you of your own capacity for excellence. Only you can. Great coaches and teammates can help, sure, but ultimately the power of success or failure, wins or losses, is on the individual.

Writing, for whatever reason, feels mystical and mysterious to many people. But working as a plumber doesn't. That's because writers have worked to make writing seem more mysterious than it is. Did you ever hear of any plumber getting plumber's block? Can you imagine if your plumber came over to your house to fix a leak, and after an hour or so he came back to you and he said, "I'm sorry. I'm just so wrapped up in my head right now that I can't fix your leak"?

You'd lose your mind if that happened. And the plumber would lose his job. But if a writer says it, you nod and pretend it's normal. It's not.

I wrote tens of thousands of words a week for years online and I never got writer's block.

Do you know why?

Because writing was my job. I had to do it if I wanted to make a living as a writer.

My grandfather, the original Clay Travis, worked in coal mines. My great-grandfather died of black lung disease in rural Kentucky. I sit in front of a computer and write words on a computer screen. If my grandfather and great-grandfather could go into a coal mine and risk their lives working there every day, you can damn sure expect that no matter what, I'm sitting down in front of this computer screen and writing every day. Writer's block is an elite pretension that presumes writing is a unique form of labor. It isn't. Writers write and workers work.

So, if you'd like to go write a book, then stop thinking about it, go stand in a bookstore in front of the section where your book would be, and then go write it.

There's my TED Talk for this chapter.

Now let's get back to work on our stories in a sentence to help define how Republicans win a landslide election in 2024.

Game of Thrones was the most popular show on television in the past ten years, right? I loved *Game of Thrones*. Well, at least until it fell completely apart in the final couple of seasons. So how would you sum up *Game of Thrones* if you had to put the entire eight-season narrative arc into a single sentence?

Pause for a moment and grab a notepad or pick up your phone and write down your one-sentence explanation of *Game of Thrones*, as if you were describing it for *TV Guide*. Don't over-think it.

Okay, here's my sentence: "Warring families in a medieval fictional universe filled with dragons and magic attempt to conquer and rule the kingdom of Westeros by sitting on the Iron Throne."

How does my sentence compare to your own?

Okay, maybe some of you are total losers and don't like sex and violence, so you have never watched it.

Well, what about *The Sopranos*? (Come to think of it, that show is also filled with sex and violence. Maybe there's a theme.)

Write your own sentence now.

Here's mine: "A middle-aged mob boss riven with insecurities, both personal and professional, battles rival mobsters in the New York City area to maintain his stature in the mob while also attempting to raise a normal family with a wife and two kids in the New Jersey suburbs."

How does this compare to your own sentence?

(If you haven't watched either *Game of Thrones* or *The Sopranos*, you really need to stop being such a huge loser.)

Okay, let's do one more. How about the best show in television history, in my always humble opinion, *Breaking Bad*?

Write your own story in a sentence.

Here's mine: "A high school chemistry teacher learns he has terminal cancer and in an effort to leave money behind for his wife and son after he dies begins to produce high-quality drugs to illegally sell in New Mexico."

There you have it, one-sentence pitches for three of the greatest TV shows ever made.

Your own sentences may be somewhat different from mine, but chances are your sentences would look somewhat similar because, after all, we're trying to get to the essence of the story that's being told.

The lesson I wanted to teach the kids in my creative writing class is that every story, whether it originates in a TV show, book, or movie, can be summed up in a single sentence. Don't overthink what you're trying to do; start with that foundational sentence and build the narrative world around it.

Every political campaign can be summed up in a single sentence as well, because political campaigns are also storytelling contests. And the candidate who tells the best story, as I told you above, wins. So let's translate my story in a one-sentence challenge to political campaigns.

How would you describe the Republican and Democratic parties and what they represent today in a single sentence? This sounds complicated, but it really isn't.

Here's my best attempt. You can write your own. Try to be objective and not overly partisan.

First, for Democrats.

"Democrats believe America is a fundamentally racist and unfair country that requires an activist government to ensure that equity prevails and no one is left behind."

And now for Republicans.

"Republicans believe that America is the freest and fairest

country in the world and needs a limited government to enforce its constitution and protect the individual freedoms of its citizens."

I think these are fairly accurate descriptions of the two political parties as they are presently constituted. What it boils down to is this: Democrats believe that America is a bad place in desperate need of reform, and Republicans believe America is a good place in desperate need of protection. That's really the essence of what Democrats and Republicans are fighting about in every election right now. (Keep in mind that what parties stand for is constantly shifting. It's why if you actually stay committed to ideals over party affiliation, then you may find yourself voting differently as you age. As I have.)

This was crystallized for me recently when I saw a man waiting in line in front of me in airport security in Detroit. He had a T-shirt with a picture of the American flag on it and the words *God Bless America*. As I was standing in line behind him, I would have been willing to bet ten thousand dollars on the spot that he had voted for Donald Trump. Purely based on the fact that he had an American flag T-shirt on.

Now, it just so happened that later on that man, who happened to be on the same flight from Detroit to Nashville as me, came over and said he was a big fan of the radio show. And I confirmed that he had voted for Trump and was a big Republican.

But I want you to just think about this for a moment—we've reached a point in time when if you have an American flag outside your house or you are simply proud to be an American, you probably vote Republican. In fact, in the twenty-first century if you simply own any American flag apparel at all, you almost certainly vote Republican.

That certainly wasn't the case when I was a kid. Yes, Walter Mondale got crushed in 1984 by Ronald Reagan, but it wasn't because he thought America was a bad place. Michael Dukakis got swamped by George H. W. Bush in 1988, but they both believed America was the greatest country in the world. Heck, that wasn't even the case when Barack Obama—whom I voted for!—ran for president in 2008 against John McCain.

In fact, Obama's entire 2008 campaign was about how amazing America was, how incredible a country it was that a mixed-race Hawaiian kid with no father at home could rise to become the president of the United States. Obama's 2008 campaign was a redo of Bill Clinton's 1992 campaign and Clinton's 1992 campaign was Reagan's 1980 campaign. All of them were rooted in optimism about the incredible and boundless opportunities of this country. There is a strong thread that connects all three of those campaigns—all three of which were large popular-vote victories—and that thread is that America is an incredible place. The campaigns that Clinton ran in 1992 and Obama ran in 2008 have become quintessentially Republican campaigns now. In fact, Democrats have gone so far left-wing that Obama's 2008 campaign, to a large degree, would be a Republican campaign today. Crazy as it may seem, in fact, Obama didn't support gay marriage in 2008 or 2012 during his presidential campaigns. Now if any person in America doesn't support gay marriage they're a horrible bigot who doesn't deserve to live in our country.

Indeed, I would argue that 2012 was the last election where

you could argue that Democrats and Republicans both believed America was the best country in the world and filled with mostly good people.

There are many fascinating reasons why this has changed—I will argue later in this book that social media has destroyed our common humanity, and I think that's the primary reason—but I just want you to think about that thesis for a moment: 2012 was the last time both parties nominated someone for president who believed America was the best country in the world.

Okay, I said you can sum up political parties in a sentence. Well, you can also sum up political campaigns in a sentence. Think about how you would sum up Donald Trump versus Hillary Clinton in 2016.

Here's my Hillary Clinton 2016 campaign in a sentence: "I'm the most qualified candidate in American history—I've been the First Lady, a senator, and secretary of state—and it's time to burst through the glass ceiling and put a woman in charge of this country."

Here's Trump's 2016 campaign in a sentence: "America is broken and I will make America great again."

Hillary's campaign, to a large extent, was about her deserving the office of the presidency based on her past experience as a politician. But it also leaned heavily on what I think was a flawed premise: identity politics. They even made this explicit by saying, "I'm with her," which said absolutely nothing at all other than Hillary was a woman. Later in this book I'm going to discuss why identity politics is the most destructive concept in my life and how Democrats took the wrong lesson from Obama's two presidential wins, but I think you'd agree these are pretty decent summaries of these 2016 campaigns in a sentence.

Now let's boil down the 2020 campaigns to a sentence apiece.

Joe Biden: "I'm not Donald Trump, and I will restore decency to the White House and normalcy to the country."

Donald Trump: "I'm going to make America even greater."

Trump lost because, thanks to Covid, many people didn't feel like America was great under his leadership. So the suggestion that he would make America greater failed to connect. Biden didn't even really offer much of an alternative—he claimed he would solve Covid, which he didn't, but mostly he just hid in his basement and claimed he wasn't Trump. The reason why Biden is so vulnerable in 2024 is that he didn't deliver on his campaign promise: America isn't normal and he hasn't restored decency to it.

Finding your story in a sentence doesn't just happen in politics. It can also happen in sports. For example, in 2000 the Baltimore Ravens, much to my chagrin as a Tennessee Titans fan, won the Super Bowl, riding one of the greatest defenses, maybe the greatest defense ever, to the title. But the Ravens' pathway to the championship wasn't smooth. In fact, at midseason it didn't look like the team was going to make the playoffs. The Ravens went the entire month of October without scoring a touchdown on offense.

Let me repeat that: the 2000 Super Bowl champion Baltimore Ravens didn't score an offensive touchdown for the entire month of October. They scored 12, 15, 3, 6, and 6 points, respectively, just 42 points in the whole month of October. That's the worst month of offensive football ever posted by a Super Bowl–winning team, and there isn't a close second.

That's when their head coach, the offensive-minded Brian Billick, decided the team would have to ride the defense. So he started calling plays differently, letting the defense dictate pace and tempo instead of the offense.

At the end of October the Baltimore Ravens were 5-4 and coming off a month where they had scored only 42 total points.

They didn't lose again for the rest of the season, running off seven straight victories in the regular season and then three straight in the playoffs. The Ravens gave up only 23 total points in four NFL playoff games (3, 10, 3, and 7), one of the best performances in NFL playoff history.

How did they do it?

They found their story in a sentence—*it's the defense, stupid.* Even though he was an offensive coach, a man labeled an offensive genius by the media, in fact Billick had to change his team's identity and embrace the talent they had, not the talent he wished they had. Once they did that, a championship followed.

Well, what should the story in a sentence be for 2024 if Republicans are going to reverse their decades of defeat? What would our landslide sentence look like for Republicans? We know what Biden and the Democrats will be selling. Democrats believe America is a racist, awful place and needs to be redeemed by an activist government to protect their identity-politics-fueled coalitions. Regardless of their candidate, that's the only message Democrats have for 2024. Well, that and that Trump (or the other candidate nominated by the Republicans) is Hitler. But claiming that everyone you don't like is Hitler has lost much of its potency, even with Democrat voters.

What's the landslide message for Republicans?

I'll tell you what it should be: "America is the greatest and freest country in the history of the world and whether you are white, black, Asian, Hispanic, gay or straight, male or female, we're going to provide support for your individual, meritocratic excellence by unlocking capitalistic expansion and make it even better for everyone."

Okay, you might be thinking, that sounds good, but what does that platform actually look like?

Let's talk about it.

But first, let me tell you more about my favorite subject—myself.

CHAPTER 3

USE THE OTHER TEAM'S PLAYBOOK AGAINST THEM

Democrats are so cocky after winning seven of the past eight presidential elections that they aren't going to change their playbook. We know exactly what they are going to do. We know their plays and we know exactly how they are going to run them.

That's actually a tremendous advantage. Because not only can we craft a playbook that works for our team, but we also don't have to worry about the Democrats changing their own playbook to adjust to what we're doing. They're so confident, they aren't changing anything at all. A big part of crafting a winning playbook is not just knowing what you want to run; it's knowing what the Democrats are going to run, too. Based on their history, and our scouting report of that history, we know exactly what plays they will run and how to beat them.

I understand that some of you, shockingly, aren't that familiar with me, and that you just bought this book because you saw a dashingly attractive stranger on the cover and thought one of two things: (1) I wish my husband was this attractive, or (2) I wish I had hair as good as this guy.

So I welcome everyone into the big tent of our 2024 landslide election playbook even if you have the tremendous misfortune of not being familiar with my incredible radio shows, my regular appearances on TV for both sports and politics, my previous best-selling books, or the incredibly influential website, Outkick.com, I founded and run.

But before we go any further, I have to be honest with all of you about my politics: I'm not a lifelong Republican. Heck, I'm not even a lifelong adult Republican. In fact, I voted for Al Gore, John Kerry, and Barack Obama in my first three presidential election years. What's more, I didn't just vote for Al Gore—I worked on his 2000 presidential campaign.

So, yeah, not only am I a recent Republican convert, but I'm a former Democrat.

And not only am I a former Democrat, I'm a former Democrat who worked in media. (Well, sports media, but it counts.) I want to be serious with you for a moment. I'm often asked how I went from working for Al Gore's presidential campaign in 2000 to voting for Donald Trump. And not just voting for Trump, but also being a robust public advocate for him.

The answer is, I haven't really changed what I believe in; the world around me has just gone insane and I've stayed sane. Ronald Reagan said, back in the 1960s when the Democrat Party went insane and he became a Republican, "I didn't leave the Democrat Party, the Democrat Party left me."

Reagan became a Republican officially in 1962 and by 1964

he was advocating strongly for the Republican presidential candidate, Barry Goldwater. Reagan ran for California governor in 1967 and won, and by 1980 he was the president of the United States.

The 1960s and our present era have much in common. Then, as now, we struggled with profound challenges about what America represented. By the end of the 1960s, left-wing excess was everywhere. That led to a massive repudiation of the Democrat Party and ushered us into a long period of stability characterized by Reagan's eight-year presidency, George H. W. Bush's win, and then Bill Clinton's presidency from 1993 to 2001. Clinton's presidency, in retrospect, was a default extension of Republican politics because Clinton governed as a moderate centrist who adopted many Republican political ideas to lead us on a mostly middle-of-the-road path into the dawn of the twenty-first century. From 1980 to 2000, the generation in which I grew up, Americans were mostly very positive about our country and our democracy. Yes, we fought about Clinton's affairs and the lies that surrounded it, but in retrospect how much less serious does a dispute over sex with an intern feel when we're talking about the FBI raiding a former president's home as he prepares for a new presidential run in 2024?

I grew up in the 1980s and the 1990s, which I'm convinced are the two greatest decades in American history. We were (mostly) peaceful in the world, communism fell, capitalism surged, democracy flourished, and people—black, white, Asian, and Hispanic—pretty much got along very well. Indeed, if you're reading this book right now and you're going to be hosting friends for food and drink and you're concerned about how every topic seems freighted with potential fights at every moment of every day, here's a great one to toss out to the table—which decade was better, the 1980s or the 1990s? My own vote? The 1990s, but most people around our age are evenly divided here. You can break everything down by movies, TV, sports, clothes, music. Just let people argue this to their heart's content and you'll have a phenomenal evening.

Maybe it's because I grew up in these two decades, but politics was characterized in those twenty years by a desire to pick someone as your presidential candidate whom you thought the other party might like. By 2016, we had repudiated this goal to such an extent that both Republicans and Democrats picked the candidate the other party hated the most as their presidential nominees, which is a tremendous departure from the politics of my childhood.

By the end of Ronald Reagan's presidency he had 60 percent approval, and so did Bill Clinton at the end of his eight years in office. How did this happen? How did we go from the 1980s and the 1990s, when two presidents from two different parties both managed to get 60 percent approval at the end of their two terms, to an era when now 50 percent approval feels like a pipe dream? Could we ever get back to that earlier era again?

I've got a provocative thesis for you. Amid the tumult of the 1960s, Richard Nixon won the election in 1968 on a platform of repudiating the excesses of the decade, and then he comfortably won reelection in 1972 on that same ideal. Then came Watergate and the accidental presidency of Jimmy Carter, who won because he wasn't the Republican (Gerald Ford). So Carter takes office and what happens? Inflation soars, the nation falls apart, interest rates for homes move up near 20 percent, and it's a complete economic cataclysm.

Jimmy Carter in 1976 is Joe Biden in 2020. Both men are accidental presidents brought on by historical abnormalities—Watergate and Covid. Look at what we have seen from Biden so far. Inflation is at a forty-year high, there is rampant runaway spending, crime is soaring, the border is a mess. Everything Biden has touched has turned to crap. He has the anti-Midas touch, the "Bidas" touch. And just like Carter, Biden is in office because of a singular event—for Carter it was Watergate, for Biden it was Covid. If Covid didn't happen in 2020, Trump would have, I believe, comfortably won reelection. Think about it: before Covid, Trump had the best economy in US history and pretty much everything was improving across the board.

Covid in 2020 was Watergate in 1976.

Both events ushered in mediocrities as presidents, historic afterthoughts.

So what happened after 1976?

Ronald Reagan rides to the rescue with a win in 1980, followed by a landslide in 1984, George H. W. Bush wins in 1988, and then Bill Clinton follows in their wake. Sure, 9/11 followed when George W. Bush was in office and that shook up the national and international experience, but the entire nation rallied around Bush, leading him to reelection in 2004 as the only Republican president since 1988 to win the popular vote. And, as I mentioned above, even Barack Obama's 2008 campaign in the wake of George W. Bush's presidency was a campaign founded on the premise that America was an incredible, amazing place to live.

After the excesses of the 1960s, we had great stability and a pro-American mindset from both parties all the way through Obama's first campaign. That's nearly forty years, two generations in fact, of relatively stable, America-is-awesome politics. Our elections up through 2008 were mostly an argument about who loved America the most and who had the best vision to ensure that we all continued to love it.

I'll grant you that 2012 was a messy campaign, but looking back on it now, how positively normal does Mitt Romney versus Barack Obama seem? You had two nerdy guys duking it out over who could nerd out more in the White House.

Then everything truly fell apart in 2016.

So let's focus on the positive here. I believe America is poised to reject the left-wing, woke overreach of our modern era just like happened in the 1960s. I believe we are set to rebound with an America-is-awesome era beginning with the 2024 election. I believe that era will extend all the way into the 2050s and may well extend through the rest of my own lifetime. I am incredibly optimistic that our modern woke-era politics are poised to come crashing down in 2024.

History doesn't repeat itself, but it often echoes. And I believe we are heading for an echo of 1980, the rise of a Ronald Reagan–like figure to unite the nation once again. Heck, we've already seen a bit of a preview in pop culture—what was the biggest movie in America in 2022? *Top Gun: Maverick*! It was the 1980s all over again. Maverick kicking the bad guys' asses and everyone leaving the theater psyched to be an American.

Plus, we know the Democrat playbook, the woke decisions that are alienating voters across the country. But they won't change. They can't. Because it keeps winning! The winning team doesn't ever adjust. That's a lesson throughout history.

Let me return to the question I began this chapter with: How did I become a Republican and how does that evolution help elucidate the failed playbook of the Democrat Party? How did a Gore campaign worker end up a huge Trump supporter, and what does that tell us about the playbook to deliver more formerly Democrat voters to a Republican landslide?

First, I don't hate America. I think America is awesome. So do the vast majority of Americans. I don't think I'm responsible for anything that my ancestors did or didn't do. I like jokes, abhor cancel culture, support a robust and uninhibited First Amendment, believe in personal freedom, think boys should play against boys and girls should play against girls in sports, support police, hate woke politics, and believe China is our greatest geopolitical threat.

Chances are, most of you agree.

And guess what? Democrats are wrong on all these issues.

Not just that, but they're proudly and committedly wrong on these issues. In fact, it's the foundation of their party now.

Even now, however, I'm a bit nervous to affiliate 100 percent with a political party because I've been burned by how insane Democrats have gone. I'm writing this book because we've lost Democrats as a party of sanity and I want to make sure that Republicans will grab this life vest and just be normal, will follow the rhythms of history and return us to a place where 60 percent of Americans can like the president and support his leadership.

But, like many of you, the Brett Kavanaugh hearings coupled with our nation's response to Covid was my crossing-the-Rubicon moment, the time when I no longer could consider myself a Democrat. The way that Democrats responded in both of these instances confirmed that their playbook was set. They are no longer the party of sanity.

The hearings for Supreme Court justice nominee Brett Kavanaugh in September 2018 were a raging embarrassment for our country. Kavanaugh was accused, at worst, of attempting to make out and fondle a girl at a drunken high school party when both were minors, way back in the early 1980s, nearly two generations ago. The absolute worst thing you can say about Kavanaugh is that when he was a teenager he tried to make out with a girl, she rejected his advances, and he behaved immaturely after that incident.

I don't even believe this account was true, but as a lawyer you are instructed to assume the truth of the allegations that are made against your client for purposes of analyzing his potential culpability. So, if you accept as truthful the allegations against Kavanaugh, guess what? They still aren't remotely criminal. No jurisdiction in the country would charge a teenage boy who got drunk and attempted to make out with an also-drunk teenage girl with sexual assault, based on the details alleged in this case. There's no way a jury would convict a teenage boy of a crime in this situation.

That's not a partisan defense of Kavanaugh. It's simply a reasoned analysis of the allegations in this situation by a lawyer who has done criminal defense work before. Any lawyer in America who had spent any time with criminal law at all could have immediately analyzed these allegations and come to the same conclusion I just did.

There were many reasons you could oppose Kavanaugh based

on his judicial philosophy, but claiming he didn't deserve to be on the Supreme Court because of the allegations made against him from back in high school is completely absurd.

Yet when I watched the Senate Judiciary Committee hearings, my jaw dropped. I couldn't believe what I was seeing. The Democrats, overrun by woke insanity, turned the entire proceeding into a kangaroo court. They were literally quizzing Kavanaugh about superlatives written in his high school yearbook in an effort to discredit his ability to sit on the Supreme Court as an adult.

In Tennessee that fall in 2018 we had a US Senate election taking place—Marsha Blackburn, a Republican congresswoman from outside Nashville, was running against Phil Bredesen, a former Democratic governor of the state. I thought Bredesen did a good job as mayor of Nashville and as governor—in fact, I'd voted for him several times before—but right then and there I made the decision I couldn't reward the Senate Democrats and add another member to their ranks. I made the choice to vote for Blackburn over Bredesen based on the Senate Kavanaugh hearings alone. (I've since gotten to know Senator Blackburn very well and been very pleased with my choice in that election.)

In particular, the Democrat senators' outlandish embrace of #MeToo made me very uncomfortable. Believing a woman because of her sex isn't justice, it's the opposite of justice. There's a reason Lady Justice is blind: because your race, sex, and ethnicity shouldn't determine whether you are being truthful or not. That's not why I went to law school. I went to law school to pursue the truth no matter where it might lead.

And to treat everyone equally under the law.

An analogy I like to use involves a book I bet almost every one of you has read, Harper Lee's *To Kill a Mockingbird.* For those of you who have forgotten, the story is this: a young girl in 1930s Alabama, Scout, whose father, Atticus Finch, is a white attorney, comes of age by witnessing the trial of a black man, Tom Robinson, who was accused of raping a white woman, Mayella Ewell.

As the trial progresses it becomes quite clear that Robinson didn't rape Mayella Ewell. Yet the jurors in the town convict Robinson anyway. It's a brutal and searing moment of reality for young Scout Finch to realize that juries don't always reach the right decision. And for many of us, especially those of us who would end up going to law school, it's a perfect distillation of why we became lawyers—to pursue the truth no matter what, to ensure that all America's citizens receive equal justice under the law.

But in *Mockingbird* truth and justice don't triumph in small-town Alabama—an all-white jury finds the black man guilty even though he's innocent. Racial animus has so corrupted the American judicial system that justice is impossible to find because all that matters is the race of the trial participants.

Fast-forward nearly one hundred years and the Senate Democrats were modern-day versions of the jury that sided with Mayella Ewell in *To Kill a Mockingbird.* They believed the woman over the man even though the evidence clearly demonstrated that the accusations couldn't be true. When you #believeallwomen, that means by default you #disbelieveallmen. That's not justice, it's injustice.

As a white man who'd attended a privileged high school, Brett Kavanaugh was an easy target, but that didn't make him any less innocent. As I reviewed all the evidence, I made the decision to publicly support Kavanaugh and to take the next step and vote for a Republican Senate candidate out of my disgust with the behavior of the Senate Democrats.

That was the beginning of my repudiation of the Democrat Party of my youth.

Then came Covid.

By 2020, I'd become disgusted with the Democrat Party's default embrace of identity politics and their decision that everything in American history was awful and racist. As a history nerd—and history major in college—I found the *New York Times'* 1619 Project and all of the critical race theory surrounding it to be particularly noxious as well.

But Covid put me over the edge.

I have three young boys, and like many of you reading this book right now, my kids are the most important things in my life. When the threat of Covid began to emerge, I read everything I could about the virus. Then one of the very first cases of Covid in the country happened in my neighborhood outside Nashville and our schools shut down in March 2020.

But by April, I was furious that any parts of our country were still shut down. The data was quite clear: young and healthy people had almost no risk from Covid. Yet even in my neighborhood, they had put up crime scene tape around our playgrounds.

Crime scene tape around playgrounds!

People were getting arrested for being on paddleboards out in the ocean, all outdoor parks were shut down, and they took rims off basketball backboards and then filled in skateboard parks with sand to keep kids from playing in them.

As each day passed and I continued to pore over the data on

Covid, I became angrier and angrier about our country being locked down.

As 20 million people lost their jobs, I felt fortunate to have a large platform, a national sports talk radio show that aired from six to nine in the morning. Ultimately, I became one of the most prominent voices in media for kids to go back to school and for sports to return. Indeed, I somehow did three hours a day of sports talk radio in March, April, May, and June with virtually zero sports going on.

I thought it was important to maintain some semblance of normalcy in a completely abnormal time. And something crazy happened during those months in the spring of 2020. Our show's audience skyrocketed. There was such a desperate demand for someone speaking sanity in an insane world that people who never listened to a sports talk radio show started listening to me because they wanted their kids to be back in school and they wanted sports to return.

They wanted our country to get back to normal, and realized that many people never wanted Covid to leave.

And that masking was insanely stupid and not supported by data, either.

What I spoke out about day after day was the importance of individual freedom. The only people I saw willing to stand with me in embracing freedom were Republican governors like Ron DeSantis of Florida. In a desperate effort to get kids back in school and return to playing sports, I got every Republican governor I could on my sports talk radio show to endorse playing college football and high school sports by the fall.

What I was saying was considered controversial, but it just seemed like common sense to me. As I said, I cared about my kids more than anything, and thankfully the data was clear that Covid wasn't a real threat to them. What was a far bigger threat was keeping kids out of school, away from their teachers and their learning environments.

The louder I spoke out against lockdowns and school shutdowns, the more vociferous the criticisms became. But I didn't care, I knew I was right. I had decided long ago, like my idol Davy Crockett before me, that once I knew I was right, I would go ahead and not worry about whether anyone was following me.

By the spring of 2020, I was a full-blown Republican. The blue state and red state responses to Covid had made me officially change political parties. I know the same thing is true for many of you. You may have relocated to a new state or put your kids in a different school because you too were so fed up with the lies you were being sold about Covid by mainstream media and by Democrats in blue cities and states.

I am convinced that in the years ahead it will be virtually impossible to find anyone who supports schools ever having been shut down, the idea of lockdowns, mask wearing, or the Covid shot mandates. Everyone who did support these measures—you're already seeing this happen—will claim no one could have known any better in 2020 and that they knew none of this made sense. Heck, you're already seeing teachers union head Randi Weingarten, who demanded schools remain closed for years for many kids, make these exact arguments. In ten or twenty years everything that I argued will be considered common sense. Already you can see the *New York Times*, *Washington Post*, CNN, and MSNBC starting to walk back their sloppy embrace of Covid restrictions.

We never should have locked down at all, period.

The combination of these two issues, the 2018 Kavanaugh hearings and the 2020 Covid response, is how I became a Republican.

I know there are many of you just like me reading this book right now. You may even feel a bit uncomfortable calling yourself a Republican because more than anything you feel like you've lost faith in the entire United States government. If our government could get so much wrong about Covid—seriously, our government would have been far better off if we'd just done the opposite of everything Dr. Fauci suggested from the moment he first opened his mouth—how can you really trust our government at all on anything?

I'm too young to have experienced it myself, but I suspect this is how many Americans felt in the wake of the Vietnam War. How could the best and brightest have gotten so much so horribly wrong? That is why I believe that Covid is my generation's Vietnam, the time when all of us with functional brains began to question the "experts" about everything.

Maybe it's the devil's advocate in me, but I've always been skeptical of people in positions of authority who claim that we need to follow their lead for our own safety. Especially when those authorities' claims lead to more expansive power for the "experts."

But here's the deal: there are tens of millions of people out there, people who haven't voted Republican at all yet, who are natural Republican voters. It's people like me who can lead to a landslide in 2024 and a long-term return to normalcy in our country.

But a landslide election requires a new Republican Party, one that truly embraces freedom and individual responsibility across many different aspects of life. That is why I'm here laying out a playbook for what that new Republican Party can look like.

Thankfully, we know exactly what the Democrat playbook will be. We have them scouted so well already that it reminds me of the end of Super Bowl XLIX in 2014, when the New England Patriots were playing the Seattle Seahawks and the Seahawks appeared to have the game won. The Seahawks were on the Patriots' one-yard line with twenty seconds to play.

That's when rookie cornerback Malcolm Butler lined up for the Patriots and, thanks to scouting, recognized the formation the Seahawks were in and correctly deduced the play they were going to run, a quick slant to the receiver. Knowing what the play was, Butler jumped in front of the pass, intercepted it, and won the Super Bowl for the Patriots. (I'm sorry for the reminder, Seahawks fans.)

Asked how he made the play after the game, Butler remarked, "From preparation. I remembered the formation they were in. . . . I just beat him [intended receiver Ricardo Lockette] to the route and made the play."

With it, Butler won the Patriots the Super Bowl.

Just like the Seahawks, the Democrats aren't disguising anything. We know exactly what plays they are going to run. We just have to stop them.

In the chapters ahead I'm going to tell you why the future of the Republican Party is multiracial and pro–legal immigration, anti-woke, in favor of free speech and a robust marketplace of ideas, anti–big tech censorship, opposed to identity politics, convinced America is the greatest country in the world thanks to our history, supportive of gay marriage and basic gay rights, anti–women in men's sports, pro-police and tough on crime, supportive of individual states being able to set abortion policies that are both pro-life and pro-choice, the party that supports comedians and jokes, and robust capitalists in favor of business.

Okay, that's a lot to digest.

You may even be shaking your head at parts of that paragraph.

But I'm not here to win an election by a tiny number of votes. I'm here to create a lasting landslide and destroy the Democrat Party as it exists today.

If that sounds like something you'd enjoy, let's begin our journey to a 2024 landslide.

CHAPTER 4

TAKE A JOKE
(AND CANCEL CANCEL CULTURE)

A big part of success in sports isn't just having the right recruits or running the right plays, it's exploiting the weaknesses of your opponent, using their flaws to further propel you to victory. If you know your opponent is weak in one area when it comes to defending you, you should exploit it as much as you possibly can.

And nowhere are Democrats weaker right now than when it comes to woke white people embracing cancel culture for comedians over jokes they don't like in particular.

It sounds crazy, but Republicans have to become the party that likes to laugh, the party that defends jokes. Let me explain further. Dave Chappelle is among the most talented comedians of his generation. But he's also managed to become one of the most controversial. How did he do so? By daring to make fun of transgender people. In a recent Netflix special Chappelle so angered the transgender community that some Netflix employees staged a walkout of the company's headquarters to protest the jokes he was telling.

Really.

Then other comedians showed up to stage a counterprotest.

What did the counterprotesters do? They carried around signs that said "We like jokes" and "Jokes are funny." The transgender protesters were so outraged by this counterprotest that they—and I can't believe this really happened—ripped the signs out of the counterprotesters' hands and destroyed them. Then they demanded security "protect" them from the people saying they liked jokes.

Democrats, and their woke white base in particular, have gone to war with comedians. Every week, it seems, another comedian comes under fire for telling "inappropriate jokes." The culture war is typically fought online, where someone tracks down jokes they find offensive and gathers a "mob" to attack these comedians for ever having the audacity to have uttered these "offensive" jokes.

Often the mobs are directed at black comedians like Chappelle and Kevin Hart, who was attacked so vociferously online for past jokes that he felt compelled to withdraw as host of the Academy Awards. But comedians of every race and both sexes have found themselves targeted. These campaigns originate online, where woke commenters, many of them initially anonymous, band together and tweet about the "unacceptable" jokes until a woke blue-checkmark member takes note of their protest, shares their tweets, writes about them, and it spills into the left-wing media as a full-blown controversy.

This is madness and indicative of the cultural rot that social media has injected into our country. But first let's talk about how our response is often backward when it comes to the way we handle these protests.

Let's begin with an analogy that I've made on my show before but I believe is perfectly illustrative of the absurd war on comedy we currently face. Pretend you were set to attend a comedy show featuring your favorite comedian at a comedy club in your hometown. I live in Nashville and there's a great comedy club on Eighth Avenue called Zanies. I've been to the Nashville Zanies many times and even done my own shows there a couple of times.

If you went to see your favorite comedian there one night and you showed up to find someone protesting outside the venue holding up a sign demanding a comedian be kept from performing in the club because the protester found his or her jokes offensive, what would you think? You'd definitely think, Man, what a loser.

You'd think the same thing if you weren't going to the comedy club. If you were driving by in your car and saw a couple of bedraggled protesters standing outside in the cold or heat or rain, you'd roll your eyes and maybe even mutter under your breath, "Get a life."

That's how almost all of us would react to someone protesting a comedian's jokes outside a comedy club.

Yet when you really think about it, at least the person protesting the club would have been willing to get dressed, get a poster board, take the time to write something on their poster board, and then spend the additional time and effort it takes to get to the club in order to protest. What's more, the protester would be willing to put their own name behind their protest, since, at least in theory, many people might recognize them and know their opinion on this issue. Then the protester would be willing to stand outside in the heat, the snow, the rain, the cold—you name it—to ensure that all of us saw what they thought of these jokes. They would have invested, at minimum, several hours in sharing their opinions with us. Yet when almost all of us saw that opinion being shared, we'd all have a nearly identical reaction: "What a loser!"

Hardly any media, if any at all, would show up to cover the protest on the local TV news or for the local paper. In general, that person protesting the comedian would be left to their own devices and almost none of us would treat them seriously at all. They'd receive almost no attention and the attention they did receive would be mostly ridicule.

Now compare that reaction to someone who is willing to invest hours and hours into making their public opinion known outside a comedy club with how we respond when someone attacks jokes online from an anonymous Twitter account. We treat the anonymous Twitter user as far more worthy of respect! Despite the fact that it truly might take two minutes for someone to dash off an opinion online from an anonymous account—and that they might well have done it from not just one anonymous account, but from dozens of anonymous accounts, since these accounts are often synced to create an artificial "controversy," which is another story entirely—almost all of us would treat that online social media opinion as more worthy of respect than the person who actually stands outside the comedy club.

That's absurd.

It's also a testament to how we've allowed our online lives to be treated more seriously than our actual in-person lives.

Republicans should become the party that always defends jokes, period.

We should oppose all cancellations of all comedians.

Sure, many of those comedians might be left-wingers, but over time that will change if Republicans consistently defend comedians from cancellation. But that's not all. Republicans should become the party that is willing to call out the online Twittersphere for what it is—mostly performative bullshit.

One of the most common questions I get asked is how people react to me in person. I'm not the kind of person to brag—remember, I'm the humblest person on the planet—but I have more than a million followers right now. Now, the truth is I should have ten million Twitter followers because I'm one of the best tweeters who has ever lived, but if you follow me on Twitter you probably have noticed that sometimes people say mean things to me online.

(Side note: When I first started writing online, I was amazed by how mean people were on the Internet. But the truth of the matter is, I've always been entertained by the hate. If I had been a pro athlete I would have enjoyed playing in front of an arena full of people who despised me as much or more than I enjoyed playing in an arena where they loved me. I've always thought there were two kinds of athletes: the ones who wanted to make plays that caused stadiums and arenas to go wild with glee and the ones who loved to hear a raucous stadium or arena suddenly go silent, where you could hear a pin drop. I've always been predisposed to the latter. It's probably the natural contrarian in me.)

I'm thankful, though, that for whatever reason, negative comments don't impact me. If ten people say something negative about me and one person says something positive, I remember the positive thing. My wife says the reason I've never needed therapy is because I get to say exactly what I believe every single day and hence have no weight on my shoulders. I think that's true, but I also think I'm helped by my generation. I'm sort of in that bridge generation, the last group of people to grow up without the Internet, yet not old enough to be clueless about it.

I was born in 1979, which means I had a normal 1980s and 1990s lifestyle before I ever got on the Internet. I didn't have an email address until college or my own computer until I was a senior in college. I grew up in the real world. But at the same time I was comfortable with how the Internet worked, so I'm not Internet clueless like someone twenty years older than me might be. I also have two feet in the media world—one online, like with Outkick and my Twitter feed, and the other more traditional media with TV and radio. That helps me balance out reactions from both spheres.

So after all those mean comments, the tens of thousands of awful things that people have said about me online, do you know how many times someone has actually come up to me in public and said something mean to my face?

Twice.

Two times in more than eighteen years of being a public figure.

Once in Knoxville, Tennessee, someone yelled at me because I'd defended Kyle Rittenhouse and said he didn't belong in jail because I believed his self-defense claim was justified, and another time in Austin, Texas, outside of the Alabama-Texas game last year when someone screamed I was a racist.

That's it.

That's the sum total of negativity I've experienced in public in eighteen years.

And it's not like I'm in hiding. I go to big college football games every weekend in the fall for Fox Sports, and I'm out in crowded bars and restaurants all over the country then, too.

It just doesn't happen, or at least in my experience, hardly at all.

That's because Twitter isn't real life; it's a carnival funhouse-mirror version of real life.

Imagine if you tried to base your diet on what you looked like in a carnival funhouse mirror. Those mirrors exaggerate your physique for laughs. You're either way skinnier or way fatter than you are in real life, you're too tall or too short, you name it. Basing your diet choices on those mirrors would be a disaster.

The same thing is true for social media: they're the carnival funhouse mirrors of life.

Yet all day long, every day in America, there are individuals and companies desperately trying to comply with the dictates of an online mob somewhere. As you're reading this today, I guarantee you there is someone, somewhere who is in the middle of being canceled for sharing their opinions.

That's why in addition to being the party that likes jokes, Republicans have to be the party that defends comedians and uses them as a metaphor to attack cancel culture. As much fun as it might be to see left-wingers canceled for what they say, I think Republicans have to stand on principle and oppose the cancellation of anyone for any shared opinion. I think that's how you win a landslide election.

SOCIAL MEDIA ADVICE
(FROM A VERY HUMBLE SOCIAL MEDIA GENIUS)

Let me take a moment to give every potential 2024 Republican candidate—as well as their staffs—advice for social media since, humbly, I'm an expert on social media. Twitter, as well as social media in general, is an important part of winning in 2024, but it's nowhere near the most important part of the playbook. It's a distraction as often as it is a difference maker.

As of this writing, I have posted more than 120,000 tweets. The number of tweets I've sent is, frankly, embarrassing. But for better or worse, every tweet I've sent has been my own words. To the best of my knowledge, I don't believe anyone has ever sent a tweet from my account other than me. (If I ever claim that I've been hacked based on something that was tweeted from my account, you can rest assured that unlike the vast majority of famous people who claim this whenever they send a controversial tweet or receive negative public attention, I've actually been hacked. And let's be honest, I might be one of the only people in the country who could be hacked and actually end up tweeting *less* controversial things than what I normally tweet.)

Earlier I talked about the artificial nature of Twitter's impact on comedy and what jokes are allowed and not allowed, but Twitter's impact on the media has been profound. In fact, it's changed the way media works. And that's occurring despite the fact that Twitter isn't much of a business. In 2021, Twitter made less than $4.5 billion in total advertising revenue. That might sound like a substantial amount, but it pales in comparison to Google, which made $209.5 billion; Facebook, which made $114.9 billion; and Amazon, which made $31.2 billion in ad revenue. Put another way, Google makes Twitter's entire yearly ad revenue every week.

What Twitter sells is the idea that everyone important is paying attention.

That's why Elon Musk was willing to pay $44 billion for the company. While I love what Elon is doing with Twitter so far, who knows what will happen on the platform, or who might even own it by the time the 2024 election season arrives in earnest.

As I've said throughout this book, I'm the humblest person I know. So take this pronouncement with that in mind: I'm incredible at Twitter.

I'm just phenomenal at using the platform to advance my interests or my company's media interests. If Twitter didn't exist, I doubt Outkick would have ever existed and you might not have been listening to me on national radio for the past several years. Twitter has been extraordinary for my career.

But it's also toxic for most people.

There is no platform with more negativity on a daily basis than Twitter. That's why it's always important to remember the number one rule of social media: it's mostly bullshit.

That is, you aren't going to win or lose a presidential campaign on social media. Look at the Democrat campaign in 2020. Do you know which campaign was the absolute worst on social media? Joe Biden's. Hell, I doubt Biden is even allowed to send a tweet. I seriously don't believe his staff would permit him to post something on his account.

But it's not just Biden.

In the 2022 primary season, Minnesota's Democrat congresswoman Ilhan Omar, who has three million Twitter followers, almost lost to Don Samuels, who has 834. Omar received 50.3 percent of the vote, Samuels got 48.2 percent of the vote, and the final margin was around 2,500 votes. If Twitter was real life, this would be impossible.

The person with millions of followers would trounce the person with hundreds of followers, but that didn't happen. Why? Because what's popular on Twitter is often not popular in the real world. While Omar may have three million followers, many of those followers aren't real and only a tiny fraction of them likely live in her district.

Plus, as Elon Musk has revealed with his Twitter Files, much of the left-wing engagement online isn't real: it's artificial, manufactured.

I've seen far too many people who believe Twitter is real life, and almost all of them end up with an artificial worldview that's far too left-wing. In fact, let's talk about who actually tweets: just 20 percent of Americans are on Twitter and only 10 percent of those 20 percent are active on it. This means much of the media narrative is set by just 2 percent of the American population.

And that 2 percent skews to the far left wing of this country.

Now, look, I'll readily acknowledge that Twitter is incredibly seductive. It makes you believe you're the most important person in the world, which everyone running for president already believes.

That's especially true when you have Twitter installed on your phone. I didn't even realize how much I looked at Twitter until one day my youngest son and I were playing cars together and he said, "Daddy, no phone."

He took my phone from my hand and put it away.

When your toddlers are noticing how much time you spend on your phone, it's a bad sign.

Twitter is an emotional medium, fantastic for reacting to live sports or live news events. But think about how often you change your mind when the emotion of the moment fades. The entire business is rigged to play to our emotions.

Why else do you think they allow favorites and retweets?

Heck, how much less interaction would Twitter receive if there wasn't the affirmation of constant feedback? Twitter is a narcissist's dream, a perpetual mirror in our pocket that's often irresistible to gaze upon.

How much different would Twitter be if our tweets were locked for twenty-four hours and didn't send until that time had passed? How many of the 120,000 tweets of mine would I have still sent? Probably many fewer. Certainly I wouldn't have sent more than a hundred thousand. Indeed, if you apply the standard of "Will this still matter in twenty-four hours?" almost none of Twitter would exist. It's an emotional, in-the-moment medium, but it's mostly ephemeral.

I used to joke that the reason I invested my money in real estate was because I made a living on the Internet and everything felt insubstantial and nonexistent there because it vanished so quickly. So I'd buy real estate, which was the exact opposite of the Internet. You could go and look at a building and be confident it existed, whereas pulling up a website article, even if you wrote it, at some times felt like it wasn't real, as if it could vanish forever at any moment. Of course, the most interesting thing about this is that many real estate guys decided to invest in the Internet for the exact opposite reason: because their brick-and-mortar properties felt antiquated next to the glitz and glamour of the information superhighway.

Sometimes, when I would contemplate the ephemerality of a day's tweets from, for instance, Donald Trump before he was banned from the site, I'd even think about Twitter in a historical context.

How, for instance, would Abraham Lincoln have used Twitter? Lincoln was famous for writing letters he never sent. When Lincoln was angry at someone, he'd write a letter, leave it in his desk, then read it the next day and decide whether to send it or not. Most of the time, he didn't send it. Why? Because his anger would be much abated a day later and he would decide the letter wasn't necessary.

Contrast that with Trump, who shared his every opinion all day long every day while he was in office. Heck, contrast that with your own social media postings. How often are they the best reflections of your personal self? If I didn't have a public media job—let's say I was teaching creative writing somewhere or practicing law—I doubt I'd tweet much, if at all.

I don't use Facebook now, for instance. I haven't logged on to it in years. If old friends want to get in touch with me, they have my cell. I've had the same number since I got my first cell phone in 2001 when I started law school. I just think most people have more to lose from Twitter than they have to gain.

How often do someone's flippant tweets from before they were in the public eye become stories once they become "famous"? It feels like almost every athlete out there tweeted something inappropriate when they were a teenager.

It's why my kids aren't allowed to have social media accounts. (That probably means, since kids are way better at technology than their parents, that my kids all have secret social media accounts we aren't smart enough to know about.)

In just a few years, Twitter has gone from a company that's mostly for fun to one that is mostly dead serious. Perhaps most significantly, what has Twitter done to our abilities to process information and analyze complex subjects? Indeed, what has Twitter done to the news itself? How has it changed all of us?

I sometimes find myself scrolling Twitter late at night when I'm in bed, seeking new news like a junkie in need of a fresh hit. One of my old bosses said he'd taken Twitter off his phone for this reason. He said it was like crack. The analogy he used was fantastic. He said the thing about crack is this: No one living in the crack house thinks the crack house is dirty, dingy, and nasty. They live there and are so addicted to the crack that they don't notice what the outside world is like.

It's a perfect analogy because just like crack, social media is addictive. Once you start, it's hard to stop. The first few times you trend on social media and the messages come pouring into you, you think everyone has an opinion about you, but then you realize most people don't care at all; it's a tiny subset of obsessives who live in that world. And the more "real" your job is, the less time you have to be scrolling on Twitter to see what the latest news is.

I personally believe that Twitter has been most beneficial to a small class of highly educated people who are online all the time. What I've been disappointed to see in particular is the degree to which otherwise smart people who are in positions of power, people who have worked their entire lives to achieve success in their careers, suddenly give up decision-making power when it comes to issues on social media.

I'm reminded of a longtime radio guy I used to work with who had been successful on the airwaves for decades in Nashville. When social media began, he refused to get a Twitter account. He'd been talking on the airwaves for three decades and always had open phone lines for callers to reach him if they wanted to share their opinions. But his young staff began to monitor the show's mentions on social media, and they would occasionally read tweets to him so he knew what people were saying.

The tweets, as tweets tend to be, were not particularly kind.

One day the host peered down at all the mentions and noticed one particularly angry tweeter. "Can you," he asked the young staffer, "reach out to this person and set up a time to talk? I don't know why he hates me so much."

Now the account, of course, was an anonymous one, not directly connected to any individual person's true identity, but the action was, I thought, so genuine and real on the part of the aging radio host that it left an impression on me. This host had spent his entire career talking to anyone who wanted to call his radio show—it's not like he'd hidden from anyone's opinions—but his natural, human reaction when he saw someone posting hateful things about him online was to want to have a conversation.

That's such a real and human request.

And it's virtually impossible to make happen.

But it hasn't stopped me from wanting to make a television show for years where anonymous haters meet face-to-face with the people they've spent years ripping online. I think it would be amazing television.

Because I'd bet you virtually everything I own that almost no one spewing vitriol online would say any of it to the person's face in an actual in-person meeting. In fact, I think the anonymous troll would almost immediately apologize for his behavior.

Which is why my number one rule for every politician running for office in 2024 is this: make sure you use social media, but don't let social media use you. That's easier said than done.

Here are three more life lessons I have for everyone on social media, especially for anyone who wants to win a landslide election in 2024.

1. Don't turn on social media notifications.

This is important. Our phones are designed to constantly grab our attention. That's their entire purpose. That's how the business works. Why do I care when someone comments on something I've said on social media? I have notifications set up for only one company on my phone—the *Wall Street Journal*.

I think the *Journal* is the best newspaper in the country. I trust them to keep me apprised of any breaking news they deem worthy of sharing that I might miss during the day. They don't spam me, and their news is fresh and relevant to what I care about.

Otherwise people I know have my cell phone number. If they have something they want to share with me, they can text it.

But even for text messages, I often turn my phone over

and turn off the sounds. Even right now as I'm writing this book, my phone is out of my reach and turned over so I can't see the screen. I'm not sure this book is worth reading anyway, but I definitely know it would be worthless if I wrote it while watching my phone screen.

2. If something trends, it's probably an outlier and not representative of the real world.

This is important.

Something's newsworthiness is typically a function of its rarity. Yet social media, due to its ubiquity, is often used to teach us the opposite. That's because anecdotal reporting has taken over in the social media age.

That viral video that you and everyone you know are sharing? It doesn't happen very often; otherwise you wouldn't be sharing it. But what often happens now, particularly in our highly polarized era, is that a viral video is shared and then people argue that it's representative of a larger truth and must be addressed via public policy.

We'll talk about Black Lives Matter (BLM) later in the book, but the George Floyd video is a perfect example of how this can create a flawed response. The reason the Floyd video was news was because it was rare. We know it's rare because police don't kill very many unarmed people— black, white, Asian, or Hispanic—in any given year.

That doesn't mean the video wasn't disturbing and powerful, but it does mean that what happened to Floyd isn't representative of what happens very often to people of any race in America. The biggest issue I see with the impact of social media on politics, and I'm going to use the Floyd example in a short while to illustrate this, is that in an effort to combat what happens in a viral video we often overreact and end up with worse policies than we had before it.

That is, it's not just that the viral video is an outlier, it's that in responding to a viral video to craft a new policy, we very often create worse outcomes than if we'd done nothing at all to respond to the video in the first place.

Think about Starbucks and their reaction to two black men being asked to leave the store because they didn't purchase anything. The long-standing Starbucks policy, which makes complete sense, is that if you're going to use their store tables, facilities, or bathrooms, you need to purchase something. Otherwise you'll be asked to leave.

This isn't rocket science. Starbucks is a business. If people who aren't consuming their products take up all the space in their store without spending money, eventually the business suffers.

But in the wake of the Starbucks story about the two black men going viral, Starbucks announced that its tables were open to all and that its bathrooms were now available to anyone in the public who wanted to use them. Fast-forward a couple of years, and what has happened? Starbucks has announced that they are closing many stores because homeless people now use the bathrooms and many customers feel unsafe in the stores because homeless people are also crowding the stores in general.

Starbucks allowed a long-standing policy that made

complete sense—people need to purchase things in the store to use the facilities—to be changed overnight based on a viral video. And that changed policy led to disaster for many Starbucks stores, ultimately resulting in the company having to close many of them.

The lesson? Don't allow anecdotal outlier videos on social media to lead you to enacting drastic changes to your existing policies.

3. Will this still matter in twenty-four hours?

This ties in well with my second lesson.

Almost nothing lasts longer than twenty-four hours on social media.

Trust me, I understand what it's like to trend and get attacked aggressively online. It's happened to me dozens of times over the years for a variety of things I've said or done. There's something about the object you carry around with you all day long—your phone—being filled with people reacting to something you said that creates a compulsion to do or say something to react to it.

But the right response almost always is just to go right on living your life. Maybe you can have fun with the fact you're trending, but almost nothing happens with the story. It just vanishes.

I know there's an entire public relations apparatus out there screaming that you have to do or say something, but the truth of the matter is that the answer to almost all social media controversy is, do less.

Because it's almost a certainty that in twenty-four

hours there will be a new story that people care about more than what you said or did, and whatever you said or did will be a distant memory.

So this is my general life advice for anyone calling you about trending: unless you're facing jail time, all publicity is good publicity.

Ultimately you should use social media like a megaphone to get your own message out and ignore everything else, especially the way people react to what you said. Another bit of good social media advice came from TV executive Jamie Horowitz, who told me several years ago that I was using social media completely wrong. The analogy he used was a perfect one: imagine if you just finished a TV show and you walked around outside asking everyone you passed on the street what they thought of you and the show you'd just been on.

It would be pathetic, right? And really weird.

Yet that's essentially what you're doing every time you go to check what people are saying on social media about you. I understand why people do it, especially those in the public eye who certainly have higher levels of narcissism than people in the general public, but that doesn't make it any less nonsensical.

A fun story: Early in my writing career online, I used to read the comments on my articles. When you're first starting out writing online, it's natural to desperately crave feedback of any kind. Even if it's negative. The first challenge of any media career, put simply, is people knowing you exist. When I first started writing online, I remember dreaming of having a hundred readers someday. A thousand was a pipe dream.

Now at Outkick and on radio and TV we have millions of people who read, listen to, or watch our content every day. But in those early days you're just hoping someone, anyone, will take note of what you said. So I would read the comments on my articles.

Like most comments on the Internet, they were frequently brutal and mean. Then something interesting happened in the comments: my mom started responding to the trolls. You can imagine my reaction. I'm scrolling through the mentions, the usual attacks happen from anonymous readers, and then, boom, MY ACTUAL MOM IS IN THE COMMENTS DEFEND- ING ME.

Talking about what a great son and husband I am, how good a dad I am. It was immediately evident this wasn't some satiri- cal fake commenter. It was really my mother, taking up arms in the comments to defend me. I stopped reading the messages and called her. I said, "Mom, you can't read anything that people say about me online anymore. And you can't respond to the people online."

My mom told me she was my mom and knew me and she wasn't going to let them say anything bad about me and also that she birthed me, so who was I to tell her what she could and couldn't do online and . . . well, you can imagine how this phone call went. Eventually she agreed to stop commenting, and to my knowledge she has stopped. (However, knowing my mom she may well have a burner account out there somewhere on the In- ternet defending me. I've been asked, by the way, whether I have any burner accounts, and the truthful answer is I'm too arrogant to let some random burner account get credit for my thoughts.

For better or worse, I attach my name to every opinion I give. Heck, I don't even think I've been anonymously quoted in any article on any subject ever before. My opinions are all brilliant. Why wouldn't I want credit for them?)

For the record, do you know who has never gotten online and defended me in the comments before?

My own wife.

She's probably just too busy.

Anyway, the realization this eventually created in me was to ignore the noise and be sure you're confident of your opinions and just keep popping them out there. If I was telling my mom not to read the comments, why in the world was *I* reading them?

Colin Cowherd, who is one of the most popular sports talk radio hosts and a good friend of mine, said he used to read the Twitter comments during his radio show commercials but eventually stopped because he realized that he was allowing those comments to influence him. People on social media might complain that you're talking about Tom Brady or LeBron James or the Cowboys too much. But the reason why anyone has any show at all is that over time they've proven to be good at talking about the topics that people care about. Why should you allow people who have no experience in building a show influence you about any topics at all? (The number one complaint that anyone in media gets: "Why are you talking about this? No one cares!" What the emailer is really saying is he doesn't care. And he's probably lying. Caring enough to email about a topic in any way means it's probably a good one. Plus, the best thing about media is we get direct data feedback on what people watch and what they read. Often people lie about both.)

The same is true for anyone in a position of prominence at a company or in elected office. If you reach the point where you have a large number of people working for you, it probably means your judgment has been pretty good. Most of the time that means you've trusted your own instincts and shown an ability to make difficult decisions. So why would you suddenly give up your own opinion of what's good or bad, right or wrong, and defer to anonymous people on social media, who aren't remotely representative of the larger American population?

Every company's social media strategy should be this: do less.

If you think you need to respond to something, wait a day. Just wait twenty-four hours. Almost every social media trending topic or "controversy" is finished in that time frame. Someone else—a person, a company, an event—will be in the crosshairs sooner than you can possibly imagine. Virtually every company or individual in the country would be better at social media if they adopted this policy.

Also, you can't make your entire persona reliable on any one platform. You can read me online at Outkick and you can buy this book. You can listen to me every day on the radio and you can watch me every day, pretty much, on Fox News. I also do a daily show on Twitter, Facebook, and YouTube. For the past several years you could also see me talk about sports gambling on FS1, and you can also watch me on Fox's college football coverage in the fall. Now, the point of this is not to point out that I'm the new King of All Media and am extraordinary at writing, radio, and TV—although of course I am. It's to point out that each of these platforms has a different audience.

The same person who recognizes me from radio might not

also recognize me from a sports gambling show. In fact, I'd venture to guess that of the millions of people who listen to me on radio, only around 5 percent of that audience is active on social media. That is, there are millions of people listening to me every day on radio who will never bother to check and see what I've tweeted.

And that's okay. That's how it should be.

It's also true for every politician and every brand active on social media.

Your audience is in the real world, and you're all too often focused on what's happening in the fake social media world. I'm not saying social media isn't important. It certainly can be fun and it's an opportunity for your brand to engage with audiences—after all, you need to be everywhere to get elected president—but social media can't be your entire strategy.

Tweet less, work more.

I'm telling you this as someone who was a social media addict for a long time. I was spending more than nine hours a day on my cell phone, most of that on social media.

NINE HOURS A DAY!

That was in addition to my daily radio shows, daily TV shows, and running Outkick. And it didn't even consider my family obligations.

Now I've dialed it back and am spending only six hours a day on my phone.

That's still a monster amount, but it's freed up an extra twenty-one hours a week for me. My goal now is to get down to four hours a day. If I manage that, I'll have freed up an extra thirty-five hours a week. That's nearly a full standard workweek that I will have cleared up in my schedule.

What will I do with all this newfound time? Well, I haven't figured that out.

But I know I'll be more productive.

Or I'll end up an alcoholic.

But I'm hoping for more productivity.

Now that I've laid out the playbook for how to handle social media, let's talk about cancel culture, which frequently plays itself out on social media.

CANCEL CANCEL CULTURE

Just before I gave my advice on social media, I said Republicans have to be the party that fights cancel culture in all its forms, using comedy as the jumping-off point. Social media and cancel culture are so deeply connected because the rise of cancel culture is inextricably intertwined with the rise of social media; it's difficult to disentangle them. The first thing we have to do is explain what cancel culture is.

Disagreeing with someone about something isn't cancel culture. That actually represents the full fruition of the marketplace of ideas. We should all feel comfortable debating with one another our differences of opinions. That's how democracy works. Our marketplace of ideas is broken thanks to the power wielded by big tech—a topic we will discuss in this book in the next chapter—but a huge part of the collapse of our national discourse is connected to cancel culture.

Defined simply, cancel culture is the difference between saying "I disagree with you because [and laying out your argument]" and "I disagree with you and you don't have the right to continue to be employed, or attend this school, or live your life as a normal human being as a result of the opinion you have shared."

I've been targeted by cancel culture for my entire professional career. I have to tell you, the first few times people try to cancel you it feels terrifying. I started off my last book with the most aggressive attempt to cancel me—the time I said on CNN that I believed in only two things completely: the First Amendment and boobs. That happened back in the fall of 2017 and is well chronicled in my bestselling book, *Republicans Buy Sneakers Too*. If you haven't read it already, what in the world are you doing with your life? Go purchase it immediately and get the full Clay Travis set (so far).

By 2017, people had been trying to cancel me for so long I was completely comfortable with the outrage brigade descending upon me over my comments on CNN. I stared down all the left-wing blue-check brigade members and emerged stronger than I had been before. Why? Because the people demanding you apologize don't ever want you to actually apologize: they want to destroy you.

The moment you apologize for what you've said, you're done. Remember the quote I shared from Charles Barkley earlier in this book? The people who like you won't defend you once you apologize, and the people who already hated you don't care that you apologized. You've managed to alienate everyone the moment you apologize for what you've said.

Now I'm not saying I'll never apologize for anything I say on radio or TV. When you're on live radio and TV for twenty-plus hours a week, you've got a lot of opportunities to misspeak, but so far I haven't ever needed to apologize for anything. That's because apologizing in public isn't a sign of strength, it's a sign of weakness. (I'm not completely anti-apology, by the way. I've been married nineteen years, so trust me, I've apologized for a bevy of things in my personal life, including, once we had kids, having to apologize for the things our kids did, too. In fact, come to think of it, my entire marriage is just one long apology.)

Sure, at this point most Republicans abhor cancel culture, but I think we can be better at standing up for everyone, yes, even if they're Democrats, when they're being canceled. It may be quaint, but I really do believe that standing on principle and precedent, even for the people who disagree with you, is how you win a landslide election. Because there are at least 20 percent of Americans who can vote one way or the other depending on the candidate. Trust me, I know. I've been one of those independent voters before.

There's a debate right now between well-intentioned conservatives about whether it makes more sense to aggressively apply cancel culture rules to left-wingers, too. (Increasingly left-wingers are now battling each other in aggressive attempts to out-woke one another and cancel each other in the process.) But I think that's the wrong direction.

Why?

Because mutual cancellation warfare doesn't lead to landslide wins.

Being right on the big issues, so correct in fact that the nation comes to support you by a magnitude of 60 percent or more, is the way to a landslide.

I believe the way to dominate, the playbook for crushing our opponents, is by defending everyone's free speech rights—yes, even liberals—and standing up for the principle that no one should lose their job over what they post on Facebook, Twitter, Instagram, or any viral video that happens to circulate online. The way to win the battle over cancel culture isn't by becoming equally censorious as the left-wing lunatics; it's by beating them on the battlefield of ideas and proving the wrongness of their positions.

And by liking jokes.

And thinking jokes are funny.

Eventually that wins the votes of black, white, Asian, and Hispanic voters, and leads to a monster multiracial landslide.

CHAPTER 5

PLAY TO YOUR STRENGTHS: FREE SPEECH

One of the most difficult challenges in sports is staying committed to your playbook and trusting it to lead you to success, especially when you know you're going to be attacked by opponents who are seeking to exploit your weaknesses.

One of the best lessons I ever heard from a coach was this: "We have to make sure we don't spend too much time worrying about what they are trying to do to us, because if we do what we're supposed to do, we're going to win. We can't get so focused on game planning for their side that we lose who we are."

That's well said. In political campaigns—and in sports—you often spend so much time worrying about the other side that you lose track of executing your own game plan. That's why it's imperative to have a core philosophy. Earlier we discussed how having an offensive and defensive philosophy is integral to success in any playbook. That's also true for political parties.

The core philosophy of the Republican Party, the single most important aspect of the party in 2024, must be to support free speech and stay committed to truth and authenticity in the marketplace of ideas, even when you know that's going to lead to withering and unfair attacks from your opponents and even when you know that big tech companies are going to be aligned against you, too.

I had to learn that lesson in my own career as well.

One of the things that happen when you become a rich, famous, and successful public figure—again, I state humbly—is that people say you've changed. That's the number one criticism you'll see about me online. "Look at Clay Travis, what a grifter he is! He doesn't believe anything that he says!"

I've always found that criticism to be particularly absurd because, if anything, I've always done the same thing in my entire media career—saying exactly what I think regardless of people's reaction to it. Talk to anyone who grew up with me or went to school with me and they'll probably say the same thing: "There's not much difference between what Clay Travis says on the radio or on TV and what he says in person."

That's so true my wife didn't listen to my radio shows for years because she was afraid of what I might say on-air and get fired. We've had many spirited discussions that she's finished by saying, "But you can't say that on-air."

In fact, the only times she has ever been really mad at me is for saying things on-air that she didn't think I should.

I'll give you an example from relatively early in my radio show career, which is probably sharing too much information, but after all, we're in the trust tree here, right? When I took my first job at Fox Sports, I had never been in a television studio before. Fox Sports hired me to come work for them when they launched FS1, which was their cable sports network to compete with ESPN. I was actually scheduled to be on the very first show that had ever aired on FS1 in August 2013, a college football season preview show with Erin Andrews, the famous sportscaster who had recruited me to Fox; Joel Klatt, the current lead analyst for Fox's college football broadcasts; Eddie George, the Heisman Trophy–winning running back from Ohio State who had, in my opinion, a hall of fame NFL career; Petros Papadakis, a former University of Southern California team captain and current Los Angeles radio host; and Mike Pereira, Fox's lead rules analyst.

The first show we taped in Fox Sports' Los Angeles studio was the first time I had ever been in a studio to do a national sports show. To say I was inexperienced in TV would be an understatement. I had no clue what I was doing.

As a result, I was nervous about the trip. Right before I was scheduled to leave for LA, I got an infected hair follicle right on the base of my penis. It was excruciatingly painful. (You can make your herpes jokes here, but it really was an infected hair follicle. I've managed to avoid herpes thanks to the fact that no one but my wife has ever wanted to sleep with me. And, truth be told, she wanted to sleep with me only when we were trying to have kids.) Worse than having the infected hair follicle on the base of my penis, which, let's be honest, is a pretty awful thing by itself, was the timing—I was afraid it might get worse and I'd have to get treatment for it in Los Angeles.

And how in the world do you find a doctor in a strange city to look at the infected hair follicle at the base of your penis? At a minimum, I'd have to tell someone on the Fox staff, people who didn't know me at all. This is right up there with the most embarrassing possible ailment you could need treatment for.

My TV career might have ended right there. Would you put a guy who had never been on television before ever on TV again if he arrived for his first day of work and immediately needed treatment for a penis ailment?

So I told my wife about it. She called the doctor here in Nashville and somehow managed to get me in to see him right before I was supposed to leave. This still meant I had to go to a doctor with this ailment here in Tennessee, which, honestly, wasn't *much* better.

As if this weren't a rough enough spot to be in, I didn't have a regular doctor who treated me since fortunately I've never really needed a doctor as an adult. (I was bitten by a German shepherd when I was six and needed fifty stitches, had my appendix out in seventh grade, and had my tonsils out after my freshman year of college, but fortunately all of those things happened before I was twenty years old and I've been a perfect image of strapping and virile healthy masculinity since then.)

As a result of my stellar health to that point, I was going in blind with my doctor. I had never seen him before, and vice versa. You know how these visits go—you have to kind of slink into the doctor's office and write your awkward health conditions on a form, then you go sit in the waiting room and try not to make eye contact with anyone, then the nurses call your name, you go to an exam room, and they give you one of those tiny paper gowns and tell you to take your clothes off and then you have to explain to an (inevitably) cute nurse about how your penis has an infected hair follicle on its base and you're trying to make sure your penis doesn't have to get amputated.

So I did all that and was sitting in one of those awkward hospital gowns that don't actually cover any of you at all and in came a doctor who asked me to show him my penis. Fortunately it was a dude—just because it would have been even more awkward if it wasn't—and so he took my balls in his hands and was palpating them around and I was worried that he was going to say I needed some sort of testicle surgery, or, God forbid, my penis was going to get amputated and I swear to God he said to me, with my cock and balls in his hands, "So tell me, is Art a real guy?"

Yep, the doctor was a listener to my Nashville sports talk radio show. So I couldn't even be the anonymous guy with the infected hair follicle on his penis. The doctor was a fan.

Now I was hosting the most popular radio show in Nashville at the time, so this wasn't that out of the blue, but I was standing there with him checking out my cock and balls while he was asking me all about the show and our callers and discussing the show in detail. I mean, he was a real listener, and all I could think was that his hands were really cold and the waiting room was really cold and he was definitely going to be telling all his friends that he saw my dick. The good news is they didn't have to amputate my penis and the doctor gave me some cream and now I'm a TV superstar with a normal, functional penis, but the bad news is I told my wife this entire story.

She thought it was really funny.

But she made me promise I wouldn't talk about any of it on the radio.

And then I talked about all of it on the radio. And now I'm

writing all about it in this book. And she's going to be mortified that I shared it all over again.

My point in sharing this entire embarrassing story is just to let you know that there isn't very much difference between what I say in the real world and what I say on the mic for my shows. I just try to be as honest as I can every day, even if that means I sometimes share embarrassing stories.

And you know what? These are the kinds of things that radio listeners remember. They forget who you picked to win the Super Bowl, but they'll remember until the day they die that I put two girls who got in a catfight at a Nashville horse race on live radio. (I still maintain this is one of the best radio segments I've ever done.)

Sometimes this brutal honesty gets me in hot water—witness the reaction when I went on CNN and said the only two things I believed in completely were the First Amendment and boobs, which I discussed earlier. The CNN host nearly had a stroke when I said that and the cancel culture mobs came after me with everything they had. But when I refused to apologize for what I said, guess what happened? Yep, the same thing that happens every time I stand by what I said: my audience got even larger.

What I've found is the more honest I am, the bigger my audience gets. Because what audiences crave more than anything is authenticity. And honesty. Whether they agree or disagree with you, if you're truthful with them, I've found, they will respect you.

For better or worse, I'm pretty much the same person I was at eighteen or twenty-two or thirty-two or forty-two.

That is why I thought it was cool when several years ago some listeners tracked down the very first thing I ever had published under my name. It was a letter to the editor I wrote when I was an eighteen-year-old freshman at George Washington University.

It was published in the student newspaper on November 17, 1997, and titled "Freedom of Speech."

My letter defended a university administrator who was being attacked by left-wingers on campus for using the phrase "rule of thumb," which the left-winger equated with the medieval idea that men could beat their wives with a stick so long as it was a thumb's width or less. Really, this was a controversy all the way back in 1997, which proves we haven't really come very far after all and that, truth be told, I've been fighting the same battles against woke political correctness my entire life.

Here's what I wrote back in the fall of 1997 in the GW student newspaper:

> I am writing in reference to the letter to the editor, "Know what you're saying" (*The GW Hatchet*, Nov. 13, p. 4) in which the writer castigates GW Vice President and treasurer Louis Katz for his use of the term "rule of thumb."
>
> The writer seems to feel that Katz somehow has insulted the student body and the university with his scurrilous vocabulary. I believe individuals such as the writer have caused members of American society to tremble when they speak in public and take offense at the most unintentional of comments.
>
> Indeed, the writer seems uncertain as to Katz's use of the phrase. She states that she is in "disbelief that a man in the highest echelon of GW's administration could actually use this

phrase and not know what he is saying." In the next paragraph, she states, "I doubt Vice President Katz even knew what he was saying."

Come now—is Katz a disrespectful "misogynistic" individual who believes that men should beat women, or is he simply answering a question about technological goals? Searching for nefarious motives within the most placid language is a sure sign that someone spends entirely too much time searching for vocabulary slights.

I support the right of Katz and any other individual to speak his mind without fear of treading upon the self-righteous toes of feminists, gays, special interest white or black groups, and any other organization seeking to find fault with honest self-expression.

The writer's overreaction should be an affront to every person who respects the basic decency of individuals and believes that every verbal usage is not an attack upon their interest group. I say use the term "rule of thumb" with reckless abandon if you wish, because I for one (and many others) will not think that you intend to denigrate women.

Aside from showing off my massive vocabulary in a letter to the editor of a student newspaper—hey, chicks dig big words—these are basically the same exact opinions I have today. Only, remember that when I wrote this I was a Democrat. Defending free speech used to be a Democrat position way back in 1997.

Which is why when I read this more than a generation after I wrote it, I love it so much. More than twenty-five years after my first published opinion, the biggest criticism that should be levied against me is that I'm still an unrequited defender of the First Amendment and of the marketplace of ideas. That is my core philosophy, my one true belief. (Well, that and that boobs are great.)

Since I made my name, at least initially, in the world of sports, the safest thing I could have done was to simply remain in sports my entire career and keep quiet about any political opinions I had. Indeed, I was offered my own TV show years ago on FS1 if I'd just shut up and talk about sports. Let me be clear—that's not a bad job. That's an incredible job. I loved talking about sports, and still do.

Just talking about sports and ignoring everything else going on in the country is essentially what Skip Bayless does at Fox Sports, and he's the highest-paid daily on-air voice at the company. He doesn't say anything about any subject other than sports. He's rewarded handsomely for it, paid tens of millions of dollars, in fact.

The same thing is true of Dan Patrick, one of the most listened-to voices in sports talk radio. Patrick has, for decades, just talked about sports. These men have made more than a hundred million dollars between them by talking only about sports. I don't begrudge them their career choices at all.

I could have just kept spouting out Jordan-versus-LeBron hot takes for decades and there would have been virtually no risk. I was guaranteed to bank tens of millions of dollars. I could have never told anyone a single political opinion I had and just pretended politics didn't exist.

I had put myself in a position where I could have become fabulously wealthy just by talking about sports. That's a job many people dream of having. Heck, it was a job I'd dreamed of having when

I started off in the sports industry. In fact, there were many years in my sports career when if you'd told me I could make six figures a year talking about sports I would have believed I hit the lottery.

But the truth of the matter, sadly, was this: I didn't even have to keep quiet about politics to make millions talking about sports. I could have done what most people in sports media do and embraced far left-wing politics, kept my jobs, and never had to worry about getting major criticism for those opinions at all. I didn't even have to be honest about my political opinions. I just had to publicly embrace the far left in this country. If I'd become a huge Bernie bro, my job security would have still been ensured forever. If I'd gone on the air and talked about how much I hated Trump and said Colin Kaepernick was the greatest hero in American history, I would have been in a perfect spot, guaranteed to be employed for life in sports media, which is even more left-wing than the traditional media.

But I wasn't willing to do that.

I couldn't just sit back and allow the country I love to descend into madness and say nothing at all about the misguided choices I believed we were making. I couldn't just stick to sports. Even if it cost me money—even if it cost me the jobs I already had—I couldn't stay quiet.

I'll discuss in more detail how sports and the real world collided for me with Covid, but just know that with sports completely shut down in March 2020 our sports talk radio show listenership surged as I fought for sports to be played that spring. It kept on growing through the 2020 presidential election and into the winter and spring of 2021.

That's when Julie Talbott, my fabulous boss at iHeartRadio,

put a really difficult decision in front of me. Did I want to switch from sports radio to politics and take over the legendary time slot of the recently deceased Rush Limbaugh, alongside Buck Sexton, a guy I'd met only once for a quick lunch? Julie was offering me the biggest job in all of radio, but it would require that I leave behind sports talk radio, one of my true loves.

I had a huge decision to make, especially since there was no risk involved in deciding to stay in sports radio.

Most people dream of getting the opportunity to take over a show like that. To be frank, I'd never had that dream. Not because I didn't respect Rush Limbaugh immensely. He's one of the two greatest radio hosts in modern history (Howard Stern, before he went woke and turned into a total pussy, is the other). But I'd spent nearly twenty years building up an audience online in the world of sports. Did I really want to leave sports behind? Not to mention there was a clear sports analogy hanging over my head—it's always tough to replace a legend. Would you really want to be the guy who took over for Bear Bryant, Vince Lombardi, Nick Saban, or Bill Belichick? Usually the later guys get run out of the business and never live up to the incredible legacy of the men they follow. They get fired in a hurry. You never want to be the guy who follows the guy in sports. You want to be the guy who follows the guy who follows the guy. That's much better job security.

But here's the deal: worrying about failure isn't healthy. Because if you only worry about failure, you don't take career chances and you don't stay committed to your core philosophies because you're letting something else dictate your decisions. That was the first lesson I'd learned in radio, back when my initial boss was terrified we'd lose our audience because I said the word *penis* too many times. Plus, if you don't take career chances, then eventually you end up unfulfilled and you create burner social media accounts and share your real opinions secretly online.

To a large extent I've been successful because I've conquered fear in my professional life. To most people the worst thing that can happen in their professional life is failure. But I've failed plenty of times. You're reading a book by a guy who once lost fifty thousand dollars trying to sell college-team-colored pants through his sports website. And that was when I didn't have the money to lose! That's when I learned that failure isn't the worst thing that can happen in your career. The worst is being so terrified of failure that you don't take any risks.

I'd still be a practicing attorney somewhere in the United States if I hadn't taken the risk to move into media. Many people thought I was crazy to turn my back on my law practice and write a book about going around to every Southeastern Conference stadium as a fan back in 2006. At the time I had no money saved up and no career prospects in the media. By 2011, when I lost my job at Fanhouse, a large Internet sports site, I was making $45,000 a year as a full-time daily radio show host in Nashville. I had two kids, ages three years and four months, respectively, and was terrified about whether I'd be able to take care of them.

I remember sitting and watching a minor-league baseball game in my hometown of Nashville convinced that I was going to end up a Triple A ballplayer, one of the guys who got so close to the major leagues they could taste it, but never was able to make it to the big leagues. That kind of failure is sometimes the most difficult, because you're so close to your ultimate goal, but you just can't get there. But that's when I realized an important lesson:

not achieving your ultimate goal isn't failure, being too scared to chase it is.

I know many of you have stared down failure in your own lives. Like me, you may have been in a position where people could look at you and consider you a failure, at a place where you worry about whether you're going to be able to take care of your family, which is one of the biggest fears any parent has. In those moments you need the internal strength to keep pushing on. You need the inner strength of faith, family, and an indomitable will to push through these obstacles. You need a core philosophy to rely on, an understanding of who you truly are.

In those times of challenge, I learned something about myself: I wasn't scared of failure, because I'd experienced failure. That helped me immensely when I had to decide whether it was time to make the move from sports to the biggest radio show in the country. Plus, this wasn't the only big decision I had to make in my professional career.

At the same time, I had to decide whether to sell my Outkick media company, which I had founded in 2011. We had several bidders and I wasn't sure what the right decision was. (Ultimately I sold Outkick to Fox in May 2021, and I've loved working there the past two years.)

During this time I had a conversation with Scott Shapiro, my boss for the past several years on my national sports talk radio show. He walked me through the opportunity and pointed out something I couldn't stop thinking about: even if I continued to grow my sports talk radio show, the largest sports talk radio show in the country would still just have a pinprick of the influence and audience of the Rush show they were offering me.

If I truly believed the country had gone insane, and everyone reading this book can clearly see that I do, how could I turn down the opportunity to help restore sanity in an insane world? How could I not want to talk to the biggest possible radio audience in America?

It was around this time that I reread that letter to the editor I'd written when I was just eighteen years old. It may sound crazy, but it was important for me to see that. Because if you're anything like me, sometimes you sit around and look at our country and wonder if maybe you're the insane person, maybe you're the one who has lost his mind and everyone else is sane. Core philosophies matter the most, in sports and life, when you're faced with the most difficult decisions.

Saying exactly what I think every day is my core value, the foundation of my career.

I took over the new radio show and haven't regretted it for one moment since. In fact, I absolutely love it. Most importantly, I've managed to remain committed to the ideals laid out in that school newspaper in 1997. If anything, the criticism of me should have been that I hadn't changed at all. I hadn't gone crazy. The world had gone crazy around me.

That insanity wasn't just happening in my radio career. It was directly playing out in the big tech world as well, where my company Outkick was under attack every day for the stories we published online.

MY BATTLE WITH BIG TECH AND THE HISTORY OF MEDIA

I wrote earlier in this chapter that your core philosophy is your guiding light. That's especially true when your core philosophy comes into direct conflict with the economic realities of running an online media business. That is exactly what happened to me with Outkick in 2020.

And it came out of this important truth:

Democrats no longer favor free speech in this country. Worse than that, they are willing to censor their political opponents by using their allies in big tech to restrict what their political opponents are allowed to say. It's truly a chilling time for anyone who believes in free speech.

The Twitter Files revelations that have surfaced since Elon Musk purchased Twitter buttressed arguments I'd been making publicly for some time. For a long time anyone who ran an online media company that didn't embrace the left wing in this country had known big tech was rigged. What Musk did was expose the smoking-gun evidence of this rig job. As someone who ran an online media outlet, Outkick.com, I knew exactly what big tech content censorship looked like. I'd experienced it myself.

That was why, in March 2021, I did something I never thought I'd do—I testified in front of Congress about the unholy alliance between big tech companies and government. The opportunity to testify forced me to think deeply about the direction of our nation and the attack upon free speech that I was seeing happen every day online.

Shortly, I'll share with you what I said to Congress that day, but before that I think it's instructive to contemplate the history of media in America. Yep, it's time for me to flex those history nerd muscles that so impressed my wife years ago when she found out about my trip to Civil War sleepaway camp.

What we are dealing with today in regard to the power of big tech isn't actually new; it's just a return to an earlier time in American media. Let me explain, humbly, as always, the entire history of American media in the next several pages. Modern American media really began with pamphlets and newspapers. You probably remember learning about Thomas Paine's seminal pamphlet arguing for American independence, *Common Sense*. *Common Sense* was the viral story of its day. So too were the Federalist Papers, the writings of Benjamin Franklin, and the Declaration of Independence amid the founding fathers era.

Before you can analyze and criticize today's media, and understand the rules that will govern the 2024 election, you need to think about how we got to where we are today. I would argue that our media today is actually more a reflection of the nineteenth century than it is an entirely new phenomenon.

A newspaper, at its most basic level, is just a business designed to make money. I know, I know, no profession in American history praises itself more than journalists, but newspapers are essentially, from a business perspective, papers designed to carry advertisements to the general public. The more people who read the news and buy the paper, the more eyes on the advertisements and hence the more money is made because more can be charged for those advertisements.

This is, in many ways, still the main model for websites even in the twenty-first century. The more people who read a site, the more money is made on it because the more eyeballs there are on advertisements.

Most newspapers, for the vast majority of our country's history, have been made up of rabidly partisan media perspectives. That is, the notion of "unbiased" journalism is a relatively recent invention in American history. For much of the eighteenth and nineteenth centuries most people got their news, if they got any written news at all, from wildly partisan newspapers.

The newspapers of those eras were essentially voices for the political parties. Democrats, Republicans, Whigs, Tories, Patriots: you name the parties that existed in those eras and there were newspapers that advocated for their policies. The papers were nakedly partisan and had, at best, a tenuous connection with the truth.

That made sense from a business perspective because you could sell your product to people who shared your worldview. In an era when many different newspapers were competing for business, you needed to have something to distinguish your brand, so you picked a political party and sold to the market that believed in that party.

But then something interesting happened, a paradigm shift in news media that offered the opportunity for more money to be made. The *New York Times* and others came up with a new, brilliant business plan. What if, instead of appealing to only one political party, the paper branded itself as an "unbiased" newspaper and put on its masthead "All the News That's Fit to Print"?

If a newspaper claimed to be providing "unbiased," "nonpartisan" news, then, at least in theory, that paper could have an even bigger audience than one that presents just one political party's views. Instead of trying to appeal to a niche, with its resulting smaller audiences, what if a newspaper attempted to appeal to as large an audience as possible? If a paper could claim to be "unbiased," then, again at least in theory, it would be able to get in front of more readers, and the paper's advertising rates, thanks to an increase in readership, would surge.

While today's *New York Times* journalists want to claim their journalism is purer than others', the truth of the matter is that arguing you were unbiased was just a great business ploy that offered a larger audience to monetize. And it worked. The *Times* slowly put more partisan newspapers out of business by taking a larger and larger share of the New York City market.

Being "nonpartisan" wasn't some grand pronouncement of journalistic ethics; it was just a really successful business plan. This business plan then spread across the country—remember, there were no national newspapers in those eras—and slowly the idea of appealing to the largest possible audience by being unaffiliated with any particular political party took root. Again, this was because the business imperatives made it the perfect plan to adopt, not because of some grand paean to journalistic ethics. Although, man, what a bonus: not only could you make more money, but you could also claim you were more morally virtuous than your competitors. A double win!

As these "nonpartisan" newspapers proliferated throughout the early part of the twentieth century, technology was evolving. Radio arose as the most powerful method of communication. And since radio, to be followed by television, relied on the government's airwaves to be distributed, the same profit imperatives—appeals to the largest possible audiences—were also readily apparent to business interests.

Politicians who recognized the power of radio to reach monster audiences more efficiently than any communication method in human history to that point restricted the ability of radio and television stations to embrace either end of the political spectrum because they were concerned that mass media would threaten their hold on power. As a result the radio business model became the same as the "nonpartisan" newspaper business—the goal was to produce content that was blandly inoffensive and appealed to the largest possible audience, thereby ensuring the largest possible revenue stream.

Many of the Federal Communications Commission (FCC) rules put in place for radio and television still exist today, even though they are quite antiquated. I'll give you an example. I'm not allowed to run for political office while hosting the *Clay & Buck* radio show. It's considered an FCC violation for a radio or TV host to run for office because the idea is that we'll have an unfair media advantage compared to whoever might run against us. That rule might well have made sense in the 1940s and 1950s when there were relatively few means of competition against a radio or TV host, but those days are long since past.

In fact, do you know what I am allowed to do? Host a podcast and run for political office!

So if I wanted to flip from being on radio to being on a podcast, I could make that switch: be a governor, senator, congressman, or president and still do my daily podcast show, too. In an era when podcast hosts are now making much more money than many radio show hosts, what sense does this make? None, honestly. That's especially the case given that in the years ahead we are rapidly advancing toward an era when all audio content will be available at all times to everyone instantaneously by many methods of distribution.

Already, many of you reading this book never listen to the traditional radio show broadcast of our show; instead you download the podcast version. Interestingly, what we've found in the data is that podcasts and radio shows work well together and don't detract, at least substantially, from the audience in either medium. Only about 10 percent of people switch back and forth between radio and podcasts. The audiences for the two mediums appear to be quite different, at least when it comes to the *Clay & Buck* show.

But if I ever run for political office, you can bet I'm not going to give up doing a daily show. Why would I? I'd probably just have to move my show to podcast in that event. And maybe someone will eventually realize how antiquated our modern FCC rules are and adjust them.

But that's for the future.

Radio nonpartisanship gave way to local TV stations, which, again, required no partisan political slant. If you're old enough to remember pre-cable-era television, you know how quaint it now seems in retrospect. What was pre-cable TV like? It appealed to the widest possible audience, both in entertainment and in news. In fact, the national TV news journalists of my youth— Tom Brokaw on NBC, Peter Jennings on ABC, and Dan Rather on CBS—were ostensibly nonpartisan purveyors of the nightly news. We know these men all had their own political opinions, but they worked quite hard to appear nonpartisan. (Rather has

since become a wildly partisan figure on Twitter, but that's of rela-
tively recent vintage, since he was cashiered in the wake of a CBS
News hit piece on George W. Bush's military service during the
Vietnam War.)

Radio and TV media from roughly the 1930s to the 1980s, a
fifty-year period of moderate news media blandness designed to
appeal to the largest possible audience, was, while the predomi-
nant experience of many of our lives, actually the outlier for most
of American media history. With the rise of cable television and
the Internet, rather than jumping into a brand-new media future,
we've actually been transported back to the eighteenth and nineteenth centuries.

Cable television, which was not a part of the public airways,
brought tons of new channels into our homes that specifically focused on individual interests. I'm a kid of the early cable era. I still
remember our family's first cable box, set up on top of our television. (This followed an ill-fated Travis family attempt at satellite
television, before we could get cable in our neighborhood.)

On the day we got cable, to pair with the VCR hooked up to
my family's sole, 1970s-era television, I remember what it was like
to suddenly be able to experience MTV, ESPN, CNN, and the
like. It was, quite simply, incredible, even though we had to stand
in front of the television and twist the dial to change the cable
channels.

My dad, a true tech Luddite to this day—he has never had an
email address—refused to get us a remote control because he was
concerned it would make us lazy. He also, and this is the complete
truth, refused to get us a dial tone phone, so we grew up with rotary telephones. (For those of you who don't know what a rotary

phone is, you had to put your finger in a hole and crank the dial around to make a call.)

When we finally got the Internet in the Travis house—the old AOL CD version—we dialed the Internet and it sounded like a rotary phone as we made that buzzing connection to the information superhighway.

Remember the "you've got mail" AOL ding?

Ah, those were the days.

The business model behind cable television began to destroy the idea of trying to reach the largest possible audience because it splintered people off into their own individual interests. Instead of the entire family gathering to watch *The Cosby Show*, the teenagers watched MTV, the parents watched CNN, and the sports fans watched ESPN. Then our news got splintered up as well. CNN, whose initial goal was to appeal to all news junkies regardless of politics—and probably saw its peak as the most trusted source in news during the Gulf War in the early 1990s—led to MSNBC and Fox News.

We have now lived in a Fox News world for more than twenty-five years. And Fox News has become, amazingly, more watched than almost any broadcast channel on television. (In 2021 Fox News was the third-most-watched channel, cable or broadcast, in the entire nation.) Indeed, television in general has essentially boiled down to news and sports. Everything else has gotten divided up even more because we've moved into an era when streaming services are destroying the cable bundle.

And what's the goal of streaming services?

To give everyone exactly what they want when they want it.

After cable came the Internet, which served to divide up the audiences in this country even further. So we've moved from a radio and TV world where everyone listened or watched to the same three or four channels to one where you have tens of thousands of entertainment options out there every single day.

Netflix founder Reed Hastings summed up the modern world by saying that Netflix was competing not with all the other channels and streaming services as much as it was with sleep. That is, until we conquer the necessity of sleep, everyone has only so many hours to spend in their day consuming media. We have reached, essentially, peak media.

And it's all a targeted niche experience.

What's interesting is that in this multiplicity of audiences, when it seems like everyone on the planet has a podcast or is an online influencer, there are actually a handful of huge winners and a gargantuan group of people with almost no audience at all. Cutting through the noise has become the biggest challenge for anyone in media.

This brings me back to news, and the profit imperatives incarnate there. Fox News, CNN, and MSNBC, the three largest news channels, make most of their money from cable and satellite subscription fees. Many people still don't realize it, but your cable or satellite fee—and right now there are still around 70 million households with cable or satellite subscriptions—is made up of individual channels, all of which receive payments, or carriage fees, as a part of the cable or satellite subscription.

ESPN is the most expensive by far at around $9 a month—go read *Republicans Buy Sneakers Too* for that boondoggle business— and Fox News is the second most expensive, at around $2 a month. CNN and MSNBC cost less. But the point is that as a result of the cable and satellite bundle, everyone with a cable or satellite subscription, regardless of their politics, is paying for Fox News, CNN, and MSNBC.

That is, the most left-wing political viewer pays for Fox News and the most right-wing political viewer pays for MSNBC. While the audiences may be niche, the payments are national. That, my friends, is a hell of a business model, because you get the benefit of the entire audience paying, but can sell specific advertising to the niche consuming your channel. The cable business, therefore, combines the best of the eighteenth- and nineteenth-century partisan newspaper business model with the mass appeal of the early-twentieth-century radio and TV business model.

Unfortunately, these cable media businesses are slowly dying.

What's replacing them is the direct subscription business, either in streaming video like Disney+, Netflix, and the like, or in media as well.

Remember those national newspapers like the *New York Times* that had identified a new business model—appealing to everyone while claiming to be nonpartisan? Well, the Internet came along and crushed their businesses. I could probably write an entire book on this, but remember classified ads? That was the single most lucrative part of the old newspaper business. It's probably how you bought a puppy, a used car, or found a roommate back in the day.

Well, Craigslist destroyed pretty much the entire classified ads business model. Why did you need to pay for an ad in the newspaper when you could put it online for virtually free?

And remember how I said the business model of a newspaper

was just to deliver ads to your front door? Well, a newspaper had a limited number of ads it could run. After all, the paper is only so many pages. But the Internet? Well, the Internet was essentially infinite.

So was its supply of ads.

Initially newspapers thought they were going to just move their ad models online. But the big newspapers realized pretty quickly that they were never going to be able to replace print dollars with digital dollars. The ad rates weren't high enough and the audiences weren't big enough.

Gulp.

Facing economic ruination, newspapers had to pivot in a hurry to save their businesses.

And what was the new savior of their business?

Online subscriptions.

The new business imperative for the *New York Times* and the *Washington Post*—subscriptions!—happened to coincide, to a large degree, with the Donald Trump presidency. Instead of trying to serve the largest possible audience and have their profit mostly driven by ad sales, the *Times* and the *Post* turned into subscription businesses, with their business goals no longer driven by what the largest audience wanted but almost entirely driven by what their subscribers wanted. (Newspaper subscriptions in the old days of daily delivery were never significant drivers of revenue. The ad dollars were always the crucial component of the business.)

What the *Times* and the *Post* rapidly discovered is that the imperative for an ad-supported business—serve the largest possible audience from an "unbiased" perspective—wasn't the same for a subscription-based business. It turns out that most newspaper subscribers to national papers like these, the people paying money online to read them, wanted partisan left-wing coverage.

They wanted the *Times* and the *Post* to destroy Trump. And Republicans in general. They wanted the papers to become mouthpieces for the political parties, partners in left-wing propaganda. They wanted the newspapers to tell them over and over that their left-wing politics made them virtuous and that their political opponents were modern-day Nazis.

In order to survive, indeed thrive, as a business, the *New York Times* and the *Washington Post* had to become partisan rags. What had been a pronounced, but relatively benign, left-wing slant for a couple of generations—a slant that may well have been a business imperative driven by the largely blue-voting audiences of those two newspapers—turned into a one-way jeremiad against truth and objectivity.

The *Times*' slogan of "All the News That's Fit to Print" turned into "All the News That's Fit to Print That Makes Trump Look Bad." I mean, this wasn't subtle. The *Post* put on their masthead "Democracy Dies in Darkness" when Donald Trump took office.

If you doubt the partisan bias, just think about this: neither the *Times* nor the *Post*, both of which covered the Trump presidency extensively, ever managed to write a popular story about Trump that was to his benefit and turned out to be untrue. Russia collusion, the Steele dossier, you name it, all of it was complete lies. But if these papers had merely been sloppy and gotten stories wrong, there would have been stories that were wrong and benefited Trump, too, right? Yet that never happened. The *Times*' and the *Post*'s failures in reporting all made Trump look worse, never better. That wasn't an accident. It was by design. It was what the business model required.

The result was that while claiming Trump's presidency was a unique threat to American democracy, the *New York Times* and the *Washington Post*, fueled by their left-wing subscribers who demanded the papers go to war with Trump, lost all trace of any notions of journalistic fair play. The failures were legion, but certainly Russian collusion, which was a total lie, yet nabbed many Pulitzers for both papers, was the epitome of the two papers' descent into partisan muck. Rather than report the truth, the papers became default propaganda arms of the Democratic National Committee.

This manifested itself quite clearly on the editorial pages of the *Times* when the paper published an opinion piece by Arkansas senator Tom Cotton calling for the National Guard to be deployed in America's cities to combat the rampant rioting and looting in the summer of 2020. When the piece ran, members of the paper's staff argued that it personally threatened them as minorities. The head of the editorial page, James Bennet, was forced to resign his post. Things had gotten so bad at the *Times* that the head of the editorial page was essentially fired for sharing an opinion, from a sitting United States senator, that the woke staffers at the paper disliked!

This was made all the worse when January 6th happened and the *Times* opinion page editors called for the National Guard to be called out to protect the Capitol, the exact same argument Senator Cotton had made roughly six months beforehand.

All of this left-wing woke activism had its roots not in actual journalistic ideals, but in the business necessity of the rapidly pivoting subscription model. To draw an interesting parallel from the world of sports, the most successful media subscription businesses online have long been team message boards. If you're a die-hard fan of a particular college football team, as I am, you often subscribe to these sites. The sites, while providing news, do so typically in an unabashed homer fashion. That is, the models of the businesses require that the fans of the teams be happy with the coverage. Since fans, generally speaking, aren't desirous of hearing how great their rival teams are and how awful their favorite team is, the sites frequently engage in boosterism and slanted coverage designed to make their fans happy. These online subscription team sites are never, for instance, going to do investigative exposés uncovering cheating by the favored team. To do so would, quite frankly, destroy the entire business model. These team sites online are advocates—fans, essentially, writing for other fans.

Since sports aren't that serious, this doesn't matter very much. Sports is, after all, the toy chest of life. People aren't checking an online team message board to discover important news about democratic institutions; they're just looking for entertainment, and boosterism, about their favorite team.

Moreover, these team sites get most of their subscribers because news on recruiting, the lifeblood of top college programs, as I mentionied above, is also driving much of this interest.

In other words, it doesn't really matter if a local Alabama or Wisconsin team site is objectively reporting on sports news featuring your favorite team, because the news isn't that important. But when you apply the same business model and the same business imperatives to politics? Well, it gets downright dangerous.

These subscription business models, which overwhelmingly are the province of left-wing media like the *New York Times* and the *Washington Post*, lead to scary groupthink. The lack of objectivity on the University of Tennessee fan site, which I'm a subscriber to, doesn't really matter very much, but when, for instance, Hunter Biden's laptop features incriminating details about Joe Biden's potential connections to Ukraine and China and it may impact his ability to win the presidency, shouldn't you report it?

Yikes.

That's a business cataclysm.

Let's put it this way: no sports team site is going to break a story that costs the team a national title or a Heisman Trophy, because the site, quite frankly, would cease to exist. Just about every subscriber would cancel their subscription.

That's why I believe the *New York Times* and the *Washington Post* behaved the way they did in October 2020 when Twitter and Facebook censored and refused to allow the *New York Post*, one of the oldest papers in America, to share its exposé on Hunter Biden's laptop and the improper Biden family business dealings located on the laptop. And when Elon Musk provided all the emails and receipts of this behavior in the winter of 2022 with his Twitter Files revelations, guess what happened? The left-wing news outlets refused to cover them.

Here we had the biggest case of censorship by major corporations in our lives—it made Watergate look like jaywalking—and the *New York Times, Washington Post*, MSNBC, CNN, ABC, CBS, and NBC all essentially refused to cover it.

Sure, most people in media producing content are unintelligent sheep—they follow wherever the leaders go—but their bosses aren't sheep. They are just following the business imperative: give the subscribers what they want. It's not just that these media companies are fundamentally dishonest and don't exist to cover the news; it's that their business models no longer permit it.

The left-wing profit incentives via subscriptions instead of advertising means total audience is no longer the goal—it's serving the audience that pays you. And the audience that pays the *New York Times* or the *Washington Post* needs to believe they are the virtuous ones, the people on the right side of history. They don't want to be presented with contradictory facts or stories that challenge their worldview; they want to have their worldview reinforced over and over again. All the news that's fit to print becomes all the news that makes you correct.

This is an important paradigm shift for Republican politicians because it means there's no real value in interacting with these media sources. They aren't interested in the truth. They're incentivized to destroy Republican politicians because that's what their business demands.

So the Mitt Romneys of the world, the Republicans desperate to be liked by these left-wing media outlets, are set up for failure. Because they're going to waste time trying to curry favor with a business model that hates them. I don't think any Republican should worry at all about trying to appeal to this audience. The moment you're a threat to the left, the moment you have a real chance to win, these outlets are going to attack you with everything they've got.

Know this, own it, and exploit their attacks.

The old days of playing nice with antagonistic media outlets are over. That might have made sense when the *New York Times* and the *Washington Post* were guilty of the usual left-wing slant. But those days are long gone. Their reporters today aren't free-thinkers, they're Democrat Party propagandists masquerading as unbiased journalists. It's a complete and total lie; don't fall for it.

If you bother to interact with these media outlets at all, and I'm not sure you should, I would do so only by recording every single question and answer on video. That way at least you'll have a full record of everything you say. Remember, they aren't reporting the news, they're trying to destroy you.

Unfortunately, many in the media, even those who lean right, are afraid of rocking the boat too much and still haven't realized the new media paradigms in play. They still think the rules of the 1980s or 1990s apply. They don't. Not at all.

We do not have an unbiased and nonpartisan news industry in this country. Pretending we do is a recipe for disaster. Indeed, while much attention—as well as derision—is often foisted upon Rupert Murdoch and his family for their leadership of Fox, it's worth contemplating for a moment this rather remarkable fact: if Murdoch didn't exist, there would be virtually no counter-programming at all against the left-wing bias in our media today. Fox News, the *Wall Street Journal*, the *New York Post*, my site Out-kick: that's essentially it when it comes to punching back against the overwhelming tide of consensus left-wing media opinion.

Whatever your opinions are of Fox, it's important to note that without Murdoch there would be virtually no marketplace of ideas in America today—we'd just have different variations of left-wing talking points, which is, quite honestly, what the left-wingers in media would prefer.

All of these thoughts were echoing in my head on March 13,

2021, when I went to Washington, DC, to testify in front of the House Judiciary Committee subcommittee that handles big tech regulations. My full testimony can be found in the appendix, but here is a sample of what I said:

On August 11th, 2020, the president of the United States, Donald Trump, joined my morning radio show, *Outkick the Coverage*, to discuss, among other things, the importance of playing college football in the fall of 2020. The president was on my show for twenty-five minutes and after the interview we posted several articles related to the interview on Outkick, the website I founded and own, which is one of the largest independent sports and opinion websites in the country.

The articles were well received by our audience because the president advocated a position both I and my site had been supporting for months: the importance of sports being played despite the challenges of Covid, college sports in particular. At the time there was massive pressure for college sports to be canceled for the fall. Indeed, within a few days of the president appearing on my show the Big Ten and Pac 12 would announce the cancellation of their fall sports seasons. Our site traffic soared on that Tuesday, setting new records as our news-breaking interview with the president of the United States reverberated across the media world.

But the next day—and for the next week—our site traffic crashed.

Why?

Because Facebook killed our traffic. Overnight our

readership vanished on their site. We lost 68 percent of our Facebook users and 76 percent of our new users on the site. . . .

The result of the lost traffic on our site was substantial— given we are paid based on the number of impressions our content receives, Facebook's alteration in our traffic after that Donald Trump interview cost us several hundred thousand dollars. In the weeks and months ahead, we tested articles with Joe Biden's name in the headline to see if there was any impact on our traffic at all.

There wasn't.

Only Trump triggered site traffic collapses on Facebook. And in the event some try to argue readers simply weren't interested in these Trump stories, this isn't true. Our site metrics proved that readers arriving from outside Facebook's walls consumed these articles even more than they did other articles on the site. This was Facebook deciding which stories their readers saw, plain and simple. . . .

Facebook is not a neutral platform and neither are most of the big tech publishers which claim neutrality. . . .

During the election big tech companies colluded and conspired to keep the *New York Post*'s story on Hunter Biden's Chinese and Ukrainian business interests from being read and shared on their site. Twitter even locked the account of the *New York Post*, one of our nation's oldest newspapers. How is this anything other than a direct editorial decision? Twitter decided it didn't like the *Post*'s content and refused to allow it to be shared.

Tech companies colluded to ensure the story wasn't widely shared on their platforms. . . .

In January 2021, Facebook, Twitter, Google, Spotify, Snapchat, Instagram, Shopify, Reddit, Twitch, YouTube, TikTok, and Pinterest all either banned or restricted the democratically elected president of the United States at the time, Donald Trump, from speaking to the country on their platforms.

The tech companies were making it very clear: they were more powerful than our nation's democracy. . . .

As a lawyer who owns a media company, I believe we have effectively ceded our nation's First Amendment rights to the titans of the tech industry. These monopolistic tech companies are so powerful—and frequently are working in such close concert with one another—that they can shut down any ideas that displease them and crush any companies that don't toe the line when it comes to supporting their practices. . . .

This is not a partisan issue.

We must have content-neutral policies in the online world and we cannot allow big tech companies to pick and choose which sides they favor, artificially impacting the marketplace of ideas in the process. It's well past time that everyone, Democrats, Republicans, and independents, recognizes the truth: big tech controls our digital lives and they aren't being held accountable for that control.

Our system for online discourse is completely rigged and totally broken.

We must change that.

Now.

My position is no less earnest today.

I never planned to become a First Amendment warrior, because

I never thought the First Amendment would ever be under assault like it is today. I also certainly never thought that if it did come under assault, it would be the left wing trying to stifle speech.

Republicans must, absolutely must, make fighting big tech censorship and a full-throated defense of the First Amendment a staple of their 2024 platform. It is the most integral and core philosophy of the party, the one issue that must be embraced no matter what. Ultimately, I sold Outkick to Fox because I believed that offered my company and our talent the best possible opportunity to fight the big tech censors and allow our voices to be heard in the marketplace of ideas.

As for me, I'm just happy that the Clay Travis of 1997 and the Clay Travis of 2023 have the exact same opinion on free speech—it's the single most important right in world history. Without it, no freedom exists.

CHAPTER 6

HELP YOUR OPPONENTS BEAT THEMSELVES

Sometimes things aren't complicated—the team you are playing has bad players, bad coaches, and a poor game plan. In situations like these, you just want to avoid getting dragged down into the mud with your opponent and letting them execute their game plan. That's exactly what's happening with the Democrat Party's embrace of identity politics, which is the most toxic American political theory of the twenty-first century.

It's rare in sports, but sometimes you *want* your opponent to execute his game plan because it's the best possible path to your own victory.

Hue Jackson was the coach of the Cleveland Browns for forty games from 2016 to 2018. During this time Jackson went—and I'm sorry for bringing this up, Browns fans—3-36-1. It's a record so improbably awful that it should be impossible to accomplish.

But the Browns did it.

Identity politics is the Cleveland Browns of American politics. Yet somehow Republicans have managed to lose to this woke nonsense that's rapidly destroying American culture and wildly unpopular. Sometimes a part of winning is just watching your opponent self-destruct. That's exactly what will happen in 2024 if Republicans address this issue correctly.

Let me dive in and explain.

In December 2022, Joe Biden had a decision to make: he could trade Viktor Bout, the so-called "Merchant of Death" who spent decades selling weapons to terrorists and dictators—weapons that were then used to kill tens of thousands of otherwise innocent people, a record of atrocity that landed Bout on the FBI's Most Wanted List—for Paul Whelan, a former US Marine who had been imprisoned in Russia for four years for a crime he denied ever committing, or he could trade Bout for Brittney Griner, an American WNBA basketball player who had refused to stand for the national anthem and requested it no longer be played before WNBA games. She had been imprisoned in Russia for ten months for being caught with hashish, a crime she admitted committing.

Who do you think Biden picked, the former soldier who had admitted no crime or the basketball player whose most prominent political statement had been that she refused to stand for the anthem? Oh, and it shouldn't matter to your answer here, but we also have to mention that Griner is a black lesbian and Whelan is a straight white man, because that's all that matters to Democrats.

Of course Biden picked Griner.

Griner's release and Whelan's continued imprisonment were a perfect illustration of the identity politics that has captured the Democrat Party. Race, gender, and sexuality are all that matter when it comes to making political decisions. Nothing else is considered.

It was the exact same political calculus that led Biden to announce that he would only pick a woman as his vice presidential running mate and to announce while campaigning for the presidency in South Carolina in the spring of 2020 that he would only pick a black woman to sit on the Supreme Court. In so doing Biden eliminated 94 percent of all Americans from consideration for the Supreme Court. He would consider only the 6 percent of the American population that was black and female for a job that 100 percent of Americans should have been considered for.

Amazingly, there was very little public outrage. Because the identity politics of the Democrat Party is so deeply embedded in our nation's consciousness, almost no one pointed out how racist and unfair this was for everyone, including the judge Biden picked, Ketanji Brown Jackson.

If Biden hadn't publicly announced he was considering only black women for the Supreme Court opening, he could have considered a full list of potential qualified judges and then picked Jackson. But he didn't do that. It wasn't enough to pick a black woman: he had to publicly announce during his campaign that he was going to do it and then reinforce that decision when he had an opportunity to pick someone for the Supreme Court. Ultimately this was condescending and belittling to Jackson herself because it delegitimized her from the moment he picked her. Biden couldn't even argue she was the best and most qualified judge. He'd stolen that moment from her with his full-on embrace of identity politics in a rank and divisive manner.

It was a profoundly racist act by a profoundly racist party.

But it was emblematic of the modern-day beliefs of the Democrat Party, which has become so racist in its overt considerations of race and gender that explicit discrimination based on race and gender is now its foundational tenet. The Democrat Party believes that minorities in this country are all victims in need of protection. This belief underscores virtually every position they take—the idea that America is irredeemably racist and only they can cure our nation of its racist past.

At its most basic level the Democrat Party has created a pyramid of victimization. The more identity politics signifiers you have, the more of a victim you are, and hence the higher you rank on this pyramid of victimization. This is why Biden chose to free Griner. Because she ranked higher on the pyramid of victimization than Whelan. Griner was black, female, and gay. It didn't matter that she had broken the law and admitted to it and been imprisoned for a far shorter length of time than Whelan, who had been imprisoned longer and maintained his innocence. Griner had to be freed because Democrats believe that Griner is the bigger victim based on her race, sex, and gender.

Identity politics is a noxious concept that has become increasingly pernicious over much of the past decade. But how did it get here? And why has it overtaken the entire Democrat Party? Well, of course, as your genius author, I have a brilliant, original theory: it has to do with Barack Obama, who broke the Democrat Party during his presidency. But not in the way many of you are thinking.

Let me explain.

As I've written earlier in the book, Obama's 2008 campaign was a love letter to the power of American exceptionalism. Obama masterfully used his own life story to chart a new narrative for America. We've long said that any person can grow up to be president in this country, but until Obama that hadn't been true for any minority. Only white men had been president.

Obama's story was captivating for many people not only because of what it meant for our country, but also because it truly led, at least in theory, to a more perfect union. An American democracy that allows all to aspire to the highest office in the land is one in which true opportunity for all exists. It's a testament to the quality of his campaign that Obama's 2008 presidential win is the only election that neither party disputed in the twenty-first century. There was an acknowledgment that Obama won because the race wasn't particularly close.

When Obama followed up that 2008 win with another in 2012, Democrats took his victory, which trumpeted a massive increase in black voter support, as a sign of a new era, a multicultural ascendancy that would win them elections for generations to come. But as we've already established, that hasn't happened. In fact, Democrats, far from solidifying their gains with minority voters, have seen those voters overwhelmingly break for Republicans since 2012. As we noted earlier in this book, Trump increased his minority support in 2020, and Asians, Hispanics, and black voters have shifted in massive numbers toward the Republican Party from 2018 to 2022 in the midterms.

Why is that?

I think it's because Obama's success broke the Democrats. What Obama represented was the triumph of a black voice in politics, but Obama didn't win because he was black, he won because he was an incredibly skilled politician, one whom Democrats, frankly, have continued to disrespect with their attempt to replicate his coalition. Obama's ascent was unique in politics, but it had already occurred in many other parts of American cultural life long before his presidency. Bill Cosby had become America's highest-paid and most-watched sitcom dad, Oprah Winfrey had become our highest-paid and most-watched talk show host, Will Smith had become America's top box-office draw, and Michael Jordan and Tiger Woods had already become America's most wealthy athletes. Leaving aside the clear tumult in Cosby's, Smith's, and Woods's recent lives, what all five of these black performers did was pave the way for Obama's political rise.

But Obama rose the same way these other five individuals did: by virtue of his individual talents. Obama triumphed in the meritocracy, not because of identity politics. (Whatever your criticisms of Obama might be, you can't fake your way to the editorship of the *Harvard Law Review*, at least not back then.) Remember, Obama went to Iowa and won the caucus there when everyone expected Hillary Clinton to be the nominee in 2008. Iowa is overwhelmingly a white state, yet Obama connected well with those white voters, so well in fact that he won an underdog campaign for the Democrat Party and then coasted to victory in 2008. Obama didn't win because he did well with black voters, he won because he did well with white voters, including white women. In fact, many white women preferred Obama over Hillary, who was supposed to be the patron saint of all women. In fact, and it's forgotten now, but black voters were actually slow to rally to Obama's support in 2008.

That's what Democrats missed with Obama: they thought he won because of his identity, but that's wrong. Obama won because his identity connected with large segments of the American population of all races, just like these five entertainers and athletes.

Indeed, one of the most frustrating parts of Donald Trump's 2016 win was how many people missed a huge story: millions of people in America voted for Obama in 2008 and 2012 and then for Trump in 2016! I've been screaming this from the rooftops for years and no one notices this. Trump won the Midwest because he flipped voters from Obama to him. While all the left-wing media was screaming about Russian collusion and racist Trump voters, what actually happened was many white voters shifted from Obama in 2012 to Trump in 2016. It seems quite unlikely that the same voters who supported a black man for president in 2008 and 2012 suddenly became white supremacists in 2016 when they supported Trump. That's the identity politics narrative we were sold, however, and as I explained earlier, it's the Achilles' heel in the Democrat playbook: they're running a game plan that flat-out doesn't work because they've misidentified the talent on their team and what leads to victory.

Think about the last fifty years in American political life. How many presidents, if they'd been able to, could have won a third term in office? Ronald Reagan would have won in 1988, Bill Clinton would have won in 2000, and Barack Obama would have won in 2016. Yet only one of their handpicked successors won an election: George H. W. Bush in 1988. That's just once in fifty years. We think of the vice president as the heir apparent to the president, but in a hundred years only one vice president has been elected to follow the president after the president served two terms. (Harry Truman and Lyndon Johnson took office, but that was after the president died.) While we think of the vice president as a likely president one day, it's not typically because he's going to be elected such.

Why is that?

If Reagan, Clinton, and Obama were so popular, why didn't their electoral popularity translate to their successors? Because, quite simply, all three men were unicorns, incredible political talents whose skill sets aren't easily replicated. That's understood when it comes to Reagan, of whom Republicans have been pining for a modern version for a generation now, and to Clinton, who even Republicans acknowledge was an incredible political talent, but I think it hasn't been readily admitted of Obama, not even by Democrats.

Instead of recognizing that Obama was a unique and transcendent political talent, Democrats took from his two presidencies the reductionist idea that they just needed a black politician on the ticket to motivate black turnout. Well, if that was true, why did Kamala Harris and Cory Booker fail so disastrously in their 2020 presidential campaigns? Heck, why did Harris, who explicitly played the race card in a Democrat debate to paint Joe Biden as a racist, end up dropping out of the presidential race before any votes had been cast? After all, wasn't she the killer app based on identity politics—a black woman who could finally unite the Obama coalition once more and break the glass ceiling?

Yet her presidential campaign failed in a disastrous fashion and her vice presidency thus far has been rooted in incompetency—so much incompetency, in fact, that Democrats are terrified to put her forward as a presidential nominee. If identity politics really was a great game plan for Democrats, then Kamala should be the most popular vice president ever. Instead, in many surveys she's the *least* popular vice president ever, at least through the first two years of a term in office.

But it's not just Kamala Harris who demonstrates the disaster of identity politics. In 2016 Hillary Clinton was also supposed to replicate the Obama coalition and finally take the White House for women and shatter the glass ceiling once and for all. Remember all those balloons that never got released at her election night party?

So what happened with Kamala and Hillary? Why couldn't they capture the Obama magic? I'll tell you: because Democrats think Obama won because of identity politics, when the truth is he won because he was a phenomenal political candidate. Obama didn't win because he was black. His race may have helped his overall narrative, but it wasn't the defining aspect of his presidency.

But Democrats are so defined by race now that they took the wrong lesson from Obama's win: it's not the race of the candidate that unites people from diverse backgrounds, it's the candidate. Americans of all races overwhelmingly reject the concept of identity politics. If this weren't true, then Kamala Harris would be president right now instead of Joe Biden. Or Hillary Clinton would have won in 2016 instead of Trump. Instead both failed.

Despite the election of an old white guy, in fact the oldest white guy to ever be elected, the noxiousness of identity politics continues to undergird the entire premise of the Biden presidency. During the campaign Biden said that any black person who voted against him wasn't black and he even promised something extraordinary, as I noted above: if he was elected, his nominee for the Supreme Court would be a black woman. We've never seen anything like this in American political history—for a candidate to announce he was limiting his search for a job to a person of a particular sex and race. (Sex alone has been used, but women make up more than half of the population.)

Minorities, particularly Asians, reject the noxious politics of affirmative action. That is why Republicans should allow Democrats to keep running their identity politics playbook: it's a disaster for Democrats. Republicans believe that all people are unique individuals, while Democrats believe every person is a prisoner of their identity. Republicans believe in the power of the individual to succeed; we believe in individual excellence and the meritocracy.

We believe our country is like sports—the best man or the best woman wins, regardless of their background. Everyone should play by the same rules, but we also understand the outcome might look different. In other words, sports competitors don't always perfectly represent the underlying racial dynamics of a country. Your identity doesn't dictate your success or failure in life; your individual talent does.

And that's okay. That's what the meritocracy is all about!

Despite what Democrats want to argue, excellence isn't defined by race. Identity politics, as practiced by Democrats, also leads to an obsession with diversity and inclusion. But it's only cosmetic diversity, based on skin color, not actual diversity, based on true diversity of thought, which is the only diversity that actually matters.

I want to hammer this home with a perfect analogy that I believe Republican politicians should adopt regularly in their 2024 stump speeches. The US men's basketball team is the best in the world, but it doesn't look like America. The team is made up entirely of black players. That's despite the fact that only 12 percent of the United States population is black.

If we insisted that our men's basketball team reflect the diversity of American life, we'd have to fire a lot of black guys. Instead of having twelve black guys on the roster, we could have only one or two. That means at least ten black guys would lose their spot on the US team. The majority of the team would need to be white, and we'd have to have Hispanic and Asian players, too. So if we wanted our basketball team to perfectly reflect the racial diversity of America, it would go from twelve black guys to seven white guys, two black guys, two Hispanic guys, and one Asian guy.

Sure, the team would be far worse and probably wouldn't win the gold medal, or maybe even any medal at all, but it would be perfectly cosmetically diverse.

Plainly, that's a ridiculous idea. In this scenario diversity isn't a strength at all, it actually makes the entire team worse. It's a weakness, not a strength. It's also unfair because it removes many of the people who are most deserving of their spots from the team, to be replaced by players of inferior talent. Put simply, sports is the last refuge of the meritocracy in American life.

The NFL is the largest and most competitive business in sports. But the NFL is also wildly lacking in American diversity on the football field. There are hardly any Hispanic or Asian players, despite the fact that Hispanic and Asian people make up around 16 percent of the American population. Just like in the upper echelons of basketball, the NFL is significantly overpopulated by black players. Indeed, roughly 68 percent of the NFL rosters are black, 25 percent are white, and Hispanics and Asians make up just 0.5 percent.

What if we argued that diversity and inclusion mandated that only 12 percent of NFL rosters could be black so that black guys weren't overrepresented in the NFL? Well, that would mean roughly eight out of every ten black players in the NFL would lose their jobs. Again, this is plainly ridiculous because we all know the NFL is an extremely competitive league and the goal is for every team to put the best players on the field. Teams aren't trying to lose games; they're maniacally pursuing the best possible talent to maximize their win totals. (This is also, by the way, why arguments that the NFL is racially biased against black quarterbacks or coaches are so laughably absurd. The NFL owners are so competitive they would hire people from any background to play quarterback or coach if it made them more likely to win. And if racism truly existed in the NFL with quarterbacks or coaches, then the teams that were the least racist, that is the teams that hired black quarterbacks or black coaches, would win far more frequently than those that did not. Plus, let's be honest, Deshaun Watson, a black quarterback who was accused of sexually assaulting more than thirty women—he settled most of the civil complaints and didn't face criminal charges—just signed the largest contract in the history of football. The largest contract in the history of football! The Watson contract by itself pretty much destroys any argument that there is racial discrimination against black quarterbacks. Especially when you consider that Jameis Winston, who also had a sexual assault allegation outstanding against him, was the number one overall draft pick a few years ago. If anyone is being discriminated against in the NFL, honestly, it's women whose sexual assault claims are pretty much ignored if the player is good enough.)

NFL teams, despite being wildly competitive and paying very high salaries to their players, are not remotely reflective of our nation's racial diversity. And guess what? That's okay! Because the best players make the team. Race should have no impact at all here. Only talent should matter. Indeed, an NFL team that perfectly represented America's racial diversity would be far worse than a team that merely sought to sign the best players. A perfectly diverse NFL team, in fact, might not even win a single game all season long. Diversity, once again, far from being a strength, would be a huge weakness when it came to winning games.

In fact, if you really want to make this example even more absurd, let's consider gender, too, and make teams even more diverse and inclusive. Because, remember, women are eligible to play in the NFL, too. They just aren't, at least so far, big enough, strong enough, or fast enough to make a team. So what if we had the wokest NFL owner of all time, an NFL owner who believed in identity politics and cosmetic diversity and followed the Democrat lead to its logical conclusion? What if that owner mandated that his team's players, in addition to being perfectly racially diverse, had to be half women, too?

Well, that team would never win a game.

And they might not ever score in a season.

And some women might die playing the game.

It would be a competitive disaster.

But the team would perfectly reflect the diversity of the country! And isn't that the most important thing!? My point here should be clear: all talent isn't evenly distributed across race and gender lines. Some racial or ethnic groups might be overrepresented in certain professions and it might have nothing at all to do with discrimination. In fact, it probably doesn't, especially not in competitive industries where making as much money as possible is the goal.

Sports is, therefore, a perfect representation of the meritocracy and of an industry that will go wherever it needs to go to find the best possible talent. The more competitive the marketplace is, in fact, the more likely an industry is to find the best man or woman for the job, because that man or woman can be the difference between victory or defeat, a thriving company or a bankrupt one.

Identity politics will eventually destroy the Democrat Party. I'm certain of it. It's completely antithetical to American individualism and ultimately leads to diversity and inclusion disasters. Identity politics also leads, as I'll show you in a few chapters, to left-wing battles because you end up with dueling identities. Who is more oppressed, a transgender woman or a black person? Good luck figuring that out. It's not just that Democrats are running a bad playbook with identity politics; it's that ultimately the players on their own teams will start feuding with each other in a modern-day oppression Olympics. Who resides at the peak of the victimization pyramid? Which means we just need to get out of the way and let them run their plays here, let them tell their story, because Americans hate it and reject it. When your opponent is running a disastrous game plan, let them keep running it! Don't stop their own idiocy from destroying them.

Democrats have lit themselves on fire with identity politics. The worst thing Republicans can do is grab a fire extinguisher and help them.

CHAPTER 7

KNOW YOUR OPPONENT'S HISTORY AS WELL AS YOU KNOW YOUR OWN

Every playbook is built on an old playbook. That's how play concepts develop. Every play stands on the shoulders of plays before it. In order to truly develop a winning strategy, you don't just need to know your opponent's playbook. You need to know where it came from. The history matters because it's there that you'll find the seeds of victory and the seeds of defeat.

One of the biggest differences between the Republicans and Democrats in today's America is how we teach history. In particular, the foundational question of history that divides the two parties is this one: Is American history a story of triumph or a tragedy? Is America a force for good or a force for evil? For most of the twentieth and twenty-first centuries, Americans of both political parties believed in the innate goodness of the American experiment. But in the past couple of decades Democrats have embraced the critical race theory, foundational belief that American history is a tragic story of a racist country. This is, in essence, the lesson of the 1619 Project, which asserts that American history began when black slaves first arrived on our shores in 1619. The 1619 Project wishes to replace the American Revolution of 1776 as our nation's founding and assert that America was founded on the original sin of slavery, and that as a result our nation's history is rooted in evil, tragedy rather than triumph, victimization as opposed to heroism.

This view of history manifests itself in all facets of American left-wing life today, including the argument in favor of reparations, which left-wingers have recently embraced and now treat as a foundational element of woke thought. Indeed, San Francisco recently suggested that every black person in the city deserves $5 million in reparations. FIVE MILLION EACH! California, a state that never allowed slavery, now believes reparations are necessary as well.

Look out, it's history nerd time and I am about to make all your pantaloons drop.

As a history nerd, here's something I never hear discussed: America had slavery as an independent country only from 1783 to 1863. That's eighty years. Slavery that existed from 1619 to 1783 was actually occurring under British colonial rule. That's 164 years. So Britain would be on the hook for two-thirds of our slavery reparations if they were actually going to be paid. Congrats, King Charles III: you waited seventy-five years to sit on the throne, and the first thing you're going to have to do is pay your old colonies trillions of dollars.

But that's not all.

Remember, African tribes sold other Africans into slavery. So reparations should also be paid by African countries. Since black slave traders were the ones who actually did the initial kidnapping in Africa, they are on the hook for a massive amount of money, too. Then you'd also have to decide who gets the reparations. What about people of mixed race? What about people who have arrived in the country since slavery ended? It's just a colossal mess, and I'm always disappointed by how little discussion there is of the British and African responsibilities here. Plus, let's be honest, why do so many people insist on pretending that slavery existed in America for only a couple of hundred years? In reality slavery has existed all over the world since the advent of humans. The truth of the matter is this: every single person reading this right now, regardless of your race, has ancestors who were slaves. The entire historical discussion about slavery is rooted in the identity politics prism we discussed in the previous chapter. It's all rooted in the myopic idea that slavery is the only issue that matters in America today and that America, somehow, is the only country with a legacy of slavery. Check out ancient Greece or Rome; heck, how about the pyramids in Egypt? Many of the most majestic historic wonders of the world were made with slave labor. Arguing in favor of reparations inevitably leads to absurdity, just like all facets of identity politics as practiced by the Democrats.

Doubt me?

One of the foremost proponents of reparations in America, Angela Davis, a black Marxist scholar of some repute and a past member of the Black Panther Party, just discovered she actually descends from the original *Mayflower* settlers. She literally had an ancestor on the *Mayflower*! Davis had white slave owners in her family tree as well. Is she going to pay reparations to herself?

Okay, now that I've history-nerded reparations to death and

proven how unworkable and absurd they truly are, one of the primary ways that woke history is crystallized these days is via a demand that monuments and memorials to American history be torn down. While initially Democrats attacked any monuments or memorials associated with the Confederacy or the Civil War, Democrats and their left-wing allies have increasingly attacked Abraham Lincoln, Ulysses Grant, even George Washington in a never-ending quest to further wokeify American history.

One of the things Donald Trump was most correct about during his presidency, in fact, was that the woke community wouldn't stop at demanding that statues of Civil War soldiers like Robert E. Lee and Stonewall Jackson be torn down. That was just the beginning of the left-wing assault upon history. These left-wing loons were definitely going to attack more of American history. Indeed, the Democrat mayor of Washington, DC, Muriel Bowser, even supported tearing down the Washington Monument and the Jefferson Memorial because both Washington and Jefferson were slaveholders.

If the wokeification of history continues, it won't be long until renaming Washington, DC, and Washington State are paramount objectives of the Democrat Party. This is how issues like this metastasize and grow. There's never any logical ending; there's always more that has to be done to sanitize American history. The slippery slope truly has no end. The woke arguments just keep growing.

Of course, this entire woke era is predicated on a huge fallacy—of judging historical figures not by their own times, but by our present times. By these standards most US historical figures, who are overwhelmingly white men, are found lacking. But what these people miss is that we, like our ancestors, will also be judged as lacking by those who come after us. It's indisputable that something virtually all of us do today will one day be considered indefensible by our descendants.

That is why the study of history demands context and nuance, two things that are increasingly in short supply in our hypercharged era. Much of our discussion about history in this country is a zero-sum game. There's a constant demand to tear down monuments and memorials, a battle that isn't about history at all, actually, but about power. But it's also reductionist as opposed to expansionist.

That is why I believe Republicans should fight these woke attacks by suggesting more historical context, not less.

As I've said, I'm a history nerd and I make no apologies for it. I even have the receipts to back it up—I mean, how many of you were badass enough to go to Civil War sleepaway camp in high school? I also majored in history in college and wrote my thesis on a subject that was so sexy, girls were regularly showing up at the library and tossing their bras at me as I wrote. My topic: What if the South had adopted a total-war mindset and burned down more northern cities during the Civil War? In particular, I focused on the community of Chambersburg, Pennsylvania, the only city the South burned during the Civil War. I compared the voting tallies from 1860 and 1864 to see whether a total-war mindset adopted by Confederate general Robert E. Lee might have led Abraham Lincoln to lose the election of 1864. In essence, was the decision of the South not to burn northern cities the right one? My analysis of the voting tallies showed that Lincoln might have lost in 1864 if the Confederacy had burned down more northern cities.

If Lincoln had lost that election, we might well be two countries right now, because George McClellan, his Democrat opponent in 1864, favored ending the war and allowing the South to secede. (I still think someone should write an entire book on this thesis, by the way. It would be a great read. And while I'm at it, will someone in Hollywood please turn the Lewis and Clark expedition into the most successful TV show in the country? If it's done well, it will dominate, trust me.)

It's probably not a coincidence, given my history nerd bona fides, that I now live, essentially, on a major Civil War battlefield in Franklin, Tennessee.

Well, just off one, anyway.

I would have been on the battlefield itself, but my wife became convinced that the house I wanted to buy, which was actually on the battlefield, was haunted.

True story.

Just what you totally expected when you bought this book. It's time for a ghost story!

Back in 2015 we made an offer on an incredible nineteenth-century home in downtown Franklin, right in the middle of the historic battlefield. The home had been a private residence for a very long time, but back at the turn of the twentieth century it had been a funeral home. Some of you might be bothered by that, but I wasn't. Most old homes have had many funerals over the years and have had many people die in them.

We didn't have a ton of money in 2015, but the housing market wasn't that hot and this home had been on the market for a decent amount of time. It was also one of those show homes and had been perfectly staged, with all the furniture and refinements laid out in exquisite style. It's the only time I've ever walked into a home and thought, I want everything exactly as it is. Just leave it like this. It's perfect. Let's buy it!

So we made an offer. The sellers countered with a higher price, as sellers generally do, and encouraged us to counter theirs and get a deal done. So it came to pass that on a cold and rainy late January evening in 2015—every time it rains in the winter it's always 34 degrees in Nashville, just a bit too warm to snow; it's awful; it was that kind of day—we took our three young kids and went back to the house to view it again and see if we wanted to make a second offer.

During our visit my wife kept complaining about the smell of the house. (I can't smell anything, so it didn't bother me.) But she kept saying it smelled moldy and asking me if I smelled anything. (My wife has asked me if I smell anything approximately a billion times in our marriage and I have never said yes. I'm convinced our house could be on fire and I'd never know it. I once got tested for allergies and was allergic to fourteen of the sixteen things they test you for. I'm even allergic to *grass*. Grass! How is this even possible?!)

Anyway, I loved this house. It was incredible, nearly seven thousand square feet, beautiful lot, with an old carriage shed out back that we were going to be able to turn into a radio studio for me.

It was nearly perfection.

We went home that night and I was ready to get this deal done and move into this other house immediately.

It was the house of my dreams.

But then all hell broke loose.

That night my wife couldn't sleep and none of the three kids could, either. Our youngest kid, still a baby, was only four months old, so he was already sleeping in a crib in our room, but our four-year-old and our seven-year-old both ended up sleeping in our bed because they had nightmares. It was pure chaos and anarchy. Even wilder than most nights are with young kids in the house.

When we woke up the next morning, my wife told me my dream house was haunted and what she had been smelling wasn't mold, it was dead bodies. She said we couldn't buy the house that I wanted to buy because it was haunted and that's why everyone had had such a bad night sleeping. Except for me. She said I slept perfect because my smelling was so bad that I couldn't smell the dead ghost bodies from inside my erstwhile dream house.

I'm not kidding. This is exactly what she told me.

What was I going to do, argue with her? And then move the entire family into a haunted house and get blamed when we all got killed by a ghost?

That morning she called our real estate agent, our friend Kelly, and pulled out of the bidding.

Our real estate agent said, "Well, I wasn't going to tell you, but after you left the people staging the house called and asked if you had young kids. I said that you did. They asked if the kids had been messing with anything in the house. I told them that I was there with you and they hadn't touched anything."

But evidently the real estate agents said they'd gone back to the house that night and all the couch cushions had been stacked one on top of the other in one of the bedrooms.

And no one else had been in the house since we left.

Dun dun dun!

Do you have goose bumps on your arms now? Not only am

I going to ensure the Republicans win the White House thanks to my political genius, but I'm also a great ghost storyteller. Let's see Mark Levin pull that off in his next book that sells a billion copies.

Whatever. I ain't afraid of no ghosts. The people who bought that house that I wanted to buy are doing fine. By which I mean none of them have been killed by ghosts. And do you know how much the home value has increased?

By three million dollars!

According to Zillow it has more than quadrupled in value since I wanted to buy it.

So those ghosts cost me millions of dollars.

Not that I'm bitter or anything.

Just down from the ghost house that my wife refused to allow our family to move into, thereby costing us millions of dollars, is a town square in downtown Franklin with a monument to Confederate soldiers that was placed there in the late 1890s. It's a single, solitary soldier atop a monument staring south, as many monuments like these do all over the South. There are also a couple of replica cannons.

In the wake of the George Floyd protests, some argued that the Confederate memorial should come down. But the local high school changed its mascot from the Rebels, and Williamson County, Tennessee, took the Confederate flag off the crest. The Confederate flag was there alongside the United States flag because of the Battle of Franklin, a significant historical event and one of the primary reasons tourists visit the county in the first place. But no: the flag was racist and couldn't be seen anywhere, even in a clear historical context referencing the Civil War.

Thankfully, despite the triumph of both of these forms of woke culture-cancellation idiocy, the Confederate soldier monument wasn't torn down. It got to stay. And do you know what was done instead? An additional monument was added to the town square. This one paid tribute to the black soldiers from Williamson County who fought for the North. Now that additional monument is located, along with plaques explaining the significance of this monument, where everyone can see it as well, just off the town square, directly in front of the old courthouse.

I'm not claiming this is a perfect way to handle all American history, but I do find it to be a great metaphor about history in general and the way we discuss it in America today. So much of our historical discussion is about tearing down monuments and memorials and very little is about adding more monuments and memorials to provide greater context and understanding to issues of immense historical complexity.

This, to me, is the best way to combat the wokeification of history.

Why can't we add more history instead of removing history? Especially because the context of the additions often adds in everyone's understanding of the overall historical landscape of our country.

Look, history is overwhelming to study. It's complicated. All of our favorite historical figures were products of the times in which they lived. They, like all of us, were enormously flawed and riddled with errors. Yet they still made the world a much better place and created the freest country in the history of the world.

Years ago I realized there were really two kinds of ways to see the world: as a zero-sum game, where there's a limited number of pie slices and everyone will fight for their slice, or as a constantly expanding pie, where everyone can have more. It seems to me that much of American history has become a version of this.

When you decide to tear down a monument or memorial, you're subscribing to the idea that there's a limited amount of history we can learn and study and that in order to do so, we have to tear down something to expand our understanding of the past. But that's actually the wrong way of thinking. We've allowed the Democrat idea of tearing down anything that offends our notions of justice today and replacing it with something more current and woke. But what this manner of thinking creates is disunity and cultural conflict.

What if instead of tearing down something, we built something new to contextualize and supplement what was already there in order to aid in everyone's understanding of the larger past conflicts in our country?

When I was a freshman in college, I went to see Taylor Branch, the author of a remarkable trilogy on the civil rights movement, *America in the King Years*, speak on the release of the third volume. Branch's trilogy is one of the greatest works of American narrative history I have read in my life. My other favorite historical trilogy is *The Civil War: A Narrative*, written by Shelby Foote. I got to meet Foote once at a Civil War conference in Tupelo, Mississippi. (I told you I was a history nerd.) When I finally summoned up the courage (I was a fifteen-year-old kid) to approach Foote, then a huge celebrity at seventy-eight years old and one of the star interviewees in Ken Burns's Civil War documentary series, and asked him to sign a copy of his book, Foote told me, "Sorry, I only sign books for close personal friends, kid."

So I was left standing there with this gigantic copy of his book and a pen.

As a fifteen-year-old kid, I remember thinking, Wow, what a jerk move. But now that I can look back on it as a grown adult, I can confidently say, "What an incredibly *dick* move." I can't remotely imagine ever turning down any kid for an autograph in any of my books. And the older I get, the more inconceivable it becomes.

Anyway, at the end of the Branch reading, I asked him to sign my copy of his book. He obliged, unlike Shelby Foote, and I told him as he signed that I had appreciated how he presented all the historical figures in his book, flaws and all.

In particular, given the surveillance of Martin Luther King Jr. that the FBI had undertaken, it was clear from the historical record that King was a serial philanderer. The FBI even sent a threatening letter to King saying they would expose these infidelities unless he committed suicide. How many people know about this at all? Most don't. After I read about this FBI surveillance of King nothing surprised me when it came to big tech and FBI collusion in our modern era. Again, we all need more history in our lives, not less!

If you read Branch's book you also learn that on the day King was shot and killed in Memphis by James Earl Ray, one of his mistresses was in his hotel room. Yet King's philandering, even as a minister, didn't distract from the power of his message during the civil rights movement.

Or from his bravery.

Branch thanked me for that response and said, "Boy, have I ever gotten a lot of criticism for that."

That interaction happened twenty-five years ago, but I still think about it when I sign books and interact with readers or listeners. You never know what kids you are speaking with or what lessons they will take from your work.

So if you're a young person reading this book, I'd like for you to take one very important lesson from this chapter: chicks dig history nerds.

Eventually.

Oh, and always sign books for young kids.

Because you never know when they may end up writing their own books one day.

Final thought: back in 1957, this question for an advice column appeared in a popular American magazine: "My problem," wrote the questioner, "is different from the ones most people have. I am a boy, but I feel about boys the way I ought to feel about girls. I don't want my parents to know about me. What can I do? Is there any place I can go for help?"

"Your problem," the answerer wrote, "is not at all an uncommon one. However, it does require careful attention. The type of feeling that you have toward boys is probably not an innate tendency, but something that has been culturally acquired. Your reasons for adopting this habit have now been consciously suppressed or unconsciously repressed. Therefore, it is necessary to deal with this problem by getting back to some of the experiences and circumstances that lead to the habit. In order to do this I would suggest that you see a good psychiatrist who can assist you in bringing to the forefront of conscience all of those experiences and circumstances that lead to the habit. You are already on the right road toward a solution, since you honestly recognize the problem and have a desire to solve it."

That advice on how to deal with attraction to men appeared in *Ebony* magazine in 1957.

The person giving the advice?

Martin Luther King Jr.

King happens to have his own memorial in Washington, DC.

By modern-day standards, King should be canceled for suggesting a gay man should get treatment for his sickness.

So, should we ignore everything that King did to make America a better place and cancel him for this transgression, demanding that his monument be pulled down for not meeting our twenty-first-century standards on homosexuality? Or should we acknowledge that King, like all of us, was imperfect, and keep his memorial standing to honor the incredible accomplishments of his life?

I think you know my answer.

But I'd love to hear the wokes answer this one.

By their own standards, MLK's statue has to come down.

Which is why sometimes the best way to win is by just letting the other side make their case to the American public.

CHAPTER 8

NEUTRALIZE YOUR OPPONENT'S STRENGTHS

Every team has talented players. A good coach will scheme up a game plan to feature those talented players. In order to win, sometimes it's important to simply limit or neutralize your opponent's strengths. In football, for instance, you might double-team a wide receiver to limit his playmaking abilities.

The same lesson applies in politics: in order to win you have to neutralize the best assets of your opposition. We've looked at issues like identity politics, cancel culture, and the wokeification of history. Republicans win on all these issues. Deep down, many Democrats know this.

That is why Democrats want to focus on different issues, in particular abortion and gay marriage. In 2022, Republicans often ignored the issue of abortion. As a result, Democrats were able to limit losses in the House and Senate. I don't think Republicans will be able to ignore these issues and win a landslide presidential election in 2024. This chapter is about how I believe both issues should be addressed.

Which means if you're reading this by the pool or on the beach, this might be where you pour yourself a fresh drink and take a deep breath.

ABORTION

Abortion is a difficult topic for many people to discuss, certainly in public.

But, amazingly, writing about abortion is far easier than talking about it live on the radio for three hours a day, which is what I've done for weeks at a time over the past couple of years.

I was at Walt Disney World's Magic Kingdom watching the fireworks show with my two youngest boys when *Politico* broke the news in May 2022 that the Supreme Court was poised to overturn *Roe v. Wade* and send the issue of abortion back to the states. I read the *Politico* story, believe it or not, while riding "It's a Small World" with my boys. I contemplated the politics of the ruling on Pirates of the Caribbean, Big Thunder Mountain, and Splash Mountain.

(Splash Mountain, of course, is the supremely racist amusement park ride that Woke Disney has decided must be torn down and replaced. I wish I was joking. Also, I apologize for enjoying the ride for the past thirty years and believing it's absurd to replace it. The original sin of Splash Mountain, by the way? It stars Brer Rabbit, who was made famous by Joel Chandler Harris, who wrote down the Uncle Remus stories, told by a former slave, in the nineteenth century. Then Disney made a movie called *Song of the South*, which is considered so racist that the company has banned it from existing almost anywhere. I watched the film recently and found it, not surprisingly, to be racist by modern-day standards, but not by the standards when it was made, in the 1940s. As I wrote in the previous chapter, rather than cancel history, I'd prefer greater contextual understanding; more, not fewer slices of historical pie. But based on a movie that almost no one ever saw, the amusement park ride is racist, and if any of you reading this right now have ever ridden Splash Mountain and enjoyed it, you're a white supremacist.)

When I got back to Nashville from Disney World, I didn't talk about my own opinion on the Supreme Court decision (*Dobbs v. Jackson Women's Health Organization*) because despite the Democrats' newfound position that men can get pregnant, I know that I never will. So I don't understand at all what being pregnant is like or what having a baby grow inside your uterus is like or how overwhelming and incredible that experience must be in all facets.

Now, I can experience it as a dad, as I have been fortunate enough to do three times. But I will never know what it's like to actually be pregnant.

So I did something I almost never do: I just started asking women their opinions on abortion. I asked all sorts of women. (And by "all sorts of women" I mean the women my wife is friends with and with whom we might be out for dinner and drinks.)

What I found was something that almost no one discusses: every single woman I talked with was both pro-life and pro-choice. That doesn't mean, significantly, that all of them didn't identify with one side or the other side of the abortion debate. It just meant that most women, when you really ask specific questions about abortion, tend to be pro-choice in the early stages of pregnancy and pro-life in the late stages.

Contrary to the idea that there's some great and massive divide on abortion with no middle ground, just about every single person in the country actually lives somewhere in the divide between fully pro-life or fully pro-choice. (When I say "fully pro-life" I mean if a pregnancy occurs for any reason, a woman has to have the baby or else a crime is committed. When I say "fully pro-choice" I mean that even if a woman is nine months pregnant and about to go into labor she can still have an abortion.) The abortion conversation in the media in this country is dominated by people who are 100 percent committed to the pro-life or pro-choice position, but what I found was almost no one is actually of that opinion. In fact, almost everyone, including me, is somewhere in between both positions: we're almost all both pro-life and pro-choice.

After these anecdotal conversations, I went to look for data on people's abortion opinions to see whether the nation had the same opinions as the women I'd spoken with. And I uncovered something significant that almost no one discusses—vast majorities of people are actually very reasonable when it comes to their opinions on abortion.

Just 10 percent of voters believe abortion should be allowed in the ninth month of pregnancy. That means 90 percent of voters disagree with Democrats who believe nine-month abortions should be permitted. Similarly, only about 10 percent of voters believe that abortion shouldn't be allowed at all. That means 90 percent of voters reject a hard-line position that there should be no abortion exceptions for rape, incest, or danger to the life of the mother, for instance. That means 80 percent of voters are somewhere in the middle, with both pro-life and pro-choice opinions depending on the week of pregnancy involved. The most common opinion of all was that abortion should be allowed up to fifteen weeks of pregnancy, or roughly in the first trimester of pregnancy, but not after that.

This is where you may need to pour yourself another drink because I'm going to tell you exactly what I think about abortion and pregnancy. That is how you know, by the way, that I'm not actually a politician, because I'd be dodging this question like Dr. Fauci testifying in Congress if I were a politician.

I personally support all rights to birth control and also hold both pro-life and pro-choice opinions when it comes to abortion. I know these opinions aren't considered acceptable and everyone has to be entirely committed to one side or the other in American life, but I'm just not. I'm not going to lie to you and claim that I'm something I'm not.

I believe abortion should be safe, legal, and rare, which used to be the Democrat position until they began to advocate for abortions in the delivery room. I also believe abortion should be permitted in the first trimester of a pregnancy. I'm open to a variety of arguments about when that right should be curtailed in the first trimester, if at all, but I also believe in abortion rights when the life of the mother, rape, or incest is involved. I also understand that the vast majority of pregnancies, well in excess of 99 percent, don't involve rape, incest, or a danger to the life of the mother. But in cases where they do, I believe abortions should be permissible.

I do not, however, believe that abortions in the third trimester should be permissible. Once you reach that stage of the pregnancy, I believe, the life of the baby should be protected. And certainly once a fetus is viable, I don't believe abortions should be performed at all.

That's it. That's my opinion.

I will now pause the book to allow you to curse me aloud, castigate me thoroughly, or send an email or tweet saying how disappointed you are that I don't have the same opinion as you.

Okay, now that you've had time to do that, let me explain my position in a larger context.

As a dad of three boys, I've been fortunate to be able to experience my wife's three pregnancies and accompany her on doctor's visits where we've found out the sex of our babies, watched them grow, plotted out due dates, and nervously awaited pre-birth tests to confirm the health of our sons. That experience developed in me a profound respect for life. Prior to going through three pregnancies with my wife, my opinion on abortion was entirely theoretical. I tended, like many young men do, to believe I was pro-choice but didn't think about it very much, if at all.

But I'd say that becoming a parent changes you, and doing so multiple times changes you even more profoundly. One reason I left sports talk radio for political talk radio, quite honestly, was that I have kids. I spend far more time thinking about what their lives are going to be like than I do thinking about my own life at this point.

Indeed, one of the things writing a book forces you to do is contemplate your own age and, frankly, your own mortality. Based on actuarial tables, I've lived over half my life now. I've got a fifteen-year-old son now. It doesn't seem that long ago that I was fifteen, and pretty soon I'm going to be out visiting colleges with my oldest son.

Last year was the twentieth anniversary of my starting law school at Vanderbilt University. They take a photo on the front steps of the school and I was looking at it recently. I was twenty-two years old when the photo was taken.

I thought it took forever to get to twenty-two years old and then I barely looked around and I was forty-two. Well, the trip to sixty-two is probably going to be even faster. It's staggering. I've loved being a parent, but I'm only ten years away from all of our kids being out of the house and away at college.

How has all of this happened so quickly?

Like many parents, we've had scary moments in our pregnancies. When my wife was pregnant with our first baby, she experienced some difficulties and we rushed to the hospital to have an ultrasound performed. At that doctor's visit they told us it was 50-50 as to whether the baby, then in his first trimester, would survive.

He did, thankfully, and today he's our eldest son, but if we had lost him, even in that early stage of pregnancy, we would have grieved a great deal.

When our second son was born, my wife had a completely drama-free pregnancy. Until the delivery. Then I watched the heart rate begin an ominous decline on the monitors in front of me and witnessed our obstetrician suddenly in a harsh and serious voice order the NICU nurses into our delivery room.

Our second son's heart rate was plummeting because the umbilical cord was caught around his neck.

I can barely describe the feeling, to go from complete joy to pure terror in an instant. I've never experienced anything like it in my life and I hope I never experience it ever again. Fortunately, our obstetrician, after about a half hour, was able to deliver our second son without issue. He's now a completely healthy twelve-year-old boy.

But I'll never forget the experience of having the NICU nurses come roaring into our delivery room and crowd around my wife's bed.

For me, our boys' lives began the moment I knew my wife was pregnant. From that point forward, if anything had happened to my wife, it wouldn't have been just her life at stake: it was our boys' lives as well. That's why I've always supported the idea that if a pregnant woman is murdered and tragically loses her child as well, it should be considered two murders.

So these are my beliefs when it comes to pregnancies. I have both pro-life and pro-choice beliefs. As do the vast majority of voters, both Republicans and Democrats.

But having been a law student, I also believe *Roe v. Wade* was a messily decided example of judicial overreach, which took away the rights of individual voters to determine what should and should not be legal in their states and instead relied upon the opinions of nine unelected justices. I believe abortion should be a political question left to be resolved by the states, not a legal question decided by judges. The *Dobbs* ruling actually allows the democratic process to play out all over the country. That is, far from being an example of democracy being subverted, *Dobbs* represents the fruition of full-fledged democracy.

As an ardent defender of federalism, I believe individual states should be able to decide abortion laws as their voters see fit. Some states will protect abortions up to nine months of pregnancy or to birth. That's a position I will reject, but I recognize that states have that authority right now. Other states may decide not to permit any abortions at all, even in cases of rape or incest. That is a position I will reject also.

From a political perspective *Dobbs* has unleashed all sorts of challenges. The Republican Party in the wake of *Dobbs* is a bit like a dog that catches a car, unsure exactly what to do with itself going forward. I believe what's needed are rational, realistic discussions focused on logic as opposed to fear.

In the 2022 election we saw that simply saying nothing on abortion was not a winning campaign strategy for Republicans. We have to address this issue head-on in campaigns because Democrats successfully motivated their base by arguing that Republicans wanted to disallow abortion everywhere, in all cases. Some Republican candidates even said they believed abortion should be considered a crime.

That's nonsense.

I think any Republican running for president has to provide a direct and transparent answer on his or her abortion position. In my opinion, the position that neutralizes Democrat attacks on abortion is this: support the right of states to make their own decisions while rejecting the extremes of both positions. The Republican candidate who will win a landslide election in 2024 will reject extremes in both directions, neither supporting no access to abortion nor allowing abortions in the ninth month of pregnancy. I believe a winning Republican candidate should also embrace federalism and allow individual states to set abortion policy. This should not be a federal issue.

This is also about messaging. I believe Republicans should attack Democrats aggressively on wanting to legalize abortions in the ninth month. That extremism is rejected by 90 percent of voters, yet it is now Democrat orthodoxy.

I believe a Republican Party that protects life for most of a pregnancy will win a landslide election in 2024 because the data reflects that the vast majority of the American public agrees with my positions here. But I think a Republican Party that doesn't address the issue at all is in danger of losing just based on the abortion issue in many swing states.

I also think there's a freedom argument at play here.

I rejected the Covid vaccine mandates because I believe in personal bodily autonomy. So do most Republicans. As I have argued for years, I don't believe the federal government should have been able to mandate the Covid shot, and I believe that anyone who lost their job because they refused to get one should get their job back, with back pay.

I believe Republicans should introduce legislation to demand that Moderna, Pfizer, and Johnson & Johnson return all the profits they made off these Covid "vaccines," which aren't vaccines at all, at least not in the traditional sense of the word. The Covid shots neither keep you from getting nor from spreading Covid. That's not a vaccine. It's at best a therapeutic. Think about it. If you got four vaccine shots for the measles and still got the measles, what would your reaction be? You'd say it was the most useless shot of all time.

We've given Pfizer, Moderna, and other drug companies tens of billions of dollars in taxpayer-funded profits for a product that didn't work. I believe the drug companies have engaged in clear fraud. They sold their shots promising they would keep you from getting or spreading Covid. But the shots didn't do that at all. No company should profit off fraud, period.

So I would demand that companies return their profits, or I would rescind their protection from lawsuits and let the plaintiff lawyers sue them to the high heavens. If there were robust investigations into these companies' behavior it would become quite clear that they all engaged in fraud, potentially of a criminal nature.

How do I square my belief in freedom of choice on Covid shots with the idea that abortion should be illegal in all circumstances? Yes, there's the argument that you're protecting the life of an unborn child in the case of abortion, so it's not completely about individual autonomy, but I think that's a hard line to thread in, for instance, the case of a sixteen-year-old who has been raped. How can I believe in the freedom to make a choice on the Covid shot and simultaneously demand that a teenage rape victim have a baby?

I just can't.

I believe the Republican Party in 2024 should be the party of freedom, and one of the most important parts is the freedom to make personal choices with your own body, whether it comes to getting the Covid shot or what to do about getting pregnant in the first few weeks of that pregnancy.

Put simply, like many of you, I wish there were no abortions at all.

I don't have any daughters and probably never will, but if I ever have a granddaughter who one day gets accidentally pregnant, I wouldn't want the state to tell her what she could or could not do in the first few weeks of her pregnancy.

Now, I understand that my abortion opinions will upset some of you, but, as I said earlier, I never look over my shoulder to see whether people agree with me or not. The reason I have the audience I do is because I tell you exactly what I think.

The truth of the matter is this: if you want to win a landslide election, you can't appeal only to one extreme position or the other on the abortion debate. Overwhelming majorities of Americans are somewhere in the middle on this issue: they aren't 100 percent pro-life or 100 percent pro-choice. Significantly, the moderate and swing voters are overwhelmingly in the middle here. They don't want to support extremists on either side.

Republicans need to protect life for the vast majority of a pregnancy, but I don't believe in zero abortion rights no matter the circumstances.

And I never will.

Now let's dive right into a really simple and noncontroversial issue—gay marriage!

GAY MARRIAGE

I've officiated two weddings in my life.

The first one ended in almost immediate divorce. The second one I thought went well, until I was told the wedding license had been rejected by the town official—in the Florida Keys!—because she was disputing my ability to officiate it.

I didn't find out about this until the bride in that ceremony, who had just had her first baby, texted me, "I think our son's a bastard because of you."

Now, no disrespect to the Florida Keys, but when I think Florida Keys, I definitely don't think about fidelity to the law and sticklers to wedding registry details. I think about naked middle-aged people having orgies while drinking piña coladas on rooftops in Key West.

So I'm 0-2 on wedding ceremonies so far.

On the positive side, my own marriage, at least so far, is still going strong at nearly twenty years. Lara and I were married in August 2004 and next year will celebrate our twentieth wedding anniversary. I learned a long time ago that successful marriages need spheres of influence. My sphere of influence is the Outkick home office. Everything else in the house is hers.

My opinion on gay marriage is simple: Republicans should stop contesting it and end this cultural battle once and for all. That's helped, at least somewhat, by the fact that Congress has now codified gay marriage as legal.

This should be considered settled law and should no longer be a contentious issue in any way.

I understand some of you disagree and feel strongly that marriage should be only between a man and a woman, but the Republican Party, if it wants to win a landslide election in 2024, needs to be the party of adult freedom when it comes to picking the adult whom you marry.

That doesn't mean you need to celebrate gay marriage or believe its legalization is the greatest moment in United States history, but its legality should no longer be challenged in any way by the Republican Party.

There have been some arguments in the wake of *Roe v. Wade* being overturned and states now having the ability to determine what abortion law should be that the entire right-to-privacy case law should be challenged. I don't believe that's true. I believe any adult should be able to marry any other adult they love and wish to commit to for their life.

Period.

That doesn't mean, however, that all issues of gay rights should be abandoned by the Republican Party.

We should, for instance, aggressively combat the idea of sexuality instruction in elementary schools—and we should continue to attack the idea that gender is a made-up social construct and anyone can be any gender they want to be at any age. But the concept of gay marriage should, again, be accepted as settled law.

As someone who has been married for nearly twenty years, I hope everyone gets married to a life partner and remains with that person for better or worse for the rest of their lives. And I would also prefer that only married people have children, since it's incredibly difficult, not to mention often economically crippling, for single parents to raise children. But we all know that doesn't happen. In fact, many of you reading this are on your second or maybe even your third marriage. Heterosexual couples long ago proved that marriage isn't sacrosanct in our culture, given the prevalence of divorce.

Yes, some gay couples will have bad marriages that end in divorce, just like some straight couples do. And, yes, some gay couples will have children and be poor parents, just like some straight couples are. But I believe the overwhelmingly most likely outcome is that gay and straight married couples won't be that different after all in the years ahead when it comes to rates of divorce.

To me, this will represent the full fruition of the marital aspiration. The data shows, again overwhelmingly, that children born in this country do far better when they are born into married households. But it's not just children who benefit from marriage. It's the adults, too.

Married couples live longer lives than nonmarried couples. (And it's not just because your spouse makes married life seem like it lasts twice as long.) Married couples really do live longer and healthier lives. This brings me to one of the biggest life lessons that I wish every politician in the country hammered home every single day—individual life choices determine whether someone succeeds or fails in America today.

In fact, did you know that if you graduate from high school, get married, get a job, and don't have a kid until you're at least twenty-five years old, your rate of poverty as an adult, no matter which racial group you're a part of or how rich or poor your parents were, is statistically zero?

I bet you didn't.

That is why any politician who wants to win a landslide in 2024 should make this a huge part of his public message. Instead of worrying about gay marriage, how about being incredibly pro-marriage overall? Think about how simple, yet also electrifying, this advice is. All of us, no matter where we start or who our parents are, can guarantee that we don't live in poverty by simply graduating from high school, getting married, getting a job, and waiting to have kids until we're twenty-five or older. Now, I hope everyone out there has far more success in life than this—I want all of you to be rich like me—but I don't think there's a single person in America who isn't capable of achieving these four goals.

We could essentially end poverty in America if every person in the country just did these four things.

We can't guarantee that anyone is going to end up rich in America based on their life choices. But we can all guarantee that we won't be poor. The data reflects that if you can avoid being poor yourself, the chances your kids will grow up poor as well are also incredibly tiny.

We should be inculcating this lesson in kids from the moment they enter school. I spend an inordinate amount of time telling my own kids this: the only hand you can rely on is the one at the end of your sleeve.

I hope everyone reading this book offers a tremendous amount of assistance to a huge variety of people you come across in your lives. I hope you've all elevated and mentored many people, not just your kids. But the truth of the matter is, you can't rely on it if you're a kid. Or an adult. In your life people are probably going to let you down.

I wish that weren't true, but it's pretty much inevitable that it will happen to all of us at some point.

Then how are you going to respond? Are you going to make yourself a victim, allow what someone else does or does not do to you or for you to dictate your future life success, or are you going to take command of your own life, determine your individual success or failure?

You have to rely on yourself, for better or worse. Self-reliance is the only path to true American freedom.

For years now I've not only done a radio show for three hours each day. I've also hosted a daily show on social media called *Out-kick the Show*. When I finish that show, I offer a bit of life advice. I typically say, "DBAP, unless you need to SBAP."

DBAP is an acronym I came up with on radio years ago. The message is simple: Don't Be A Pussy. We've since sold tens of thousands of these shirts, and many of you, including me, have taken this as a simple life motto. Why? Because I think it resonates with many. Life requires risk; life requires that you take a chance. Intelligent risk analysis is, I believe, the single best attribute that determines whether someone is a success or failure in life.

But no suggestion is bulletproof.

Especially not with men involved. There's a reason no woman's final two words are ever "Watch this!" Men—or boys—for thousands of years have been engaging in risky behavior in an effort to attract attention, often from the fairer sex. That is why there are tens of thousands of men, across thousands of years, whose final two spoken words have been "Watch this!"

Which brings us to the second part of our important life lesson, "DBAP, unless you need to SBAP." What does SBAP stand for? Sometimes Be A Pussy.

Not all risks are worth taking.

For instance, if you find yourself standing on the shore of a crocodile-infested river and someone dares you to swim across it, you should probably decline. And if someone tries to shame you into swimming across the river by calling you a pussy, you can rightly respond, "SBAP, bro."

Now, you might be wondering, how did endorsing gay marriage turn into a meditation on risk and individual responsibility? The answer is, I see them as one and the same. A 2024 Republican landslide must give all adults the freedom to make good and bad decisions in their life. Republicans must be the party of personal freedom in 2024.

I don't want the government telling me whom I can marry or restricting my individual ability to embrace life success and take risks.

However, that doesn't mean *all* freedoms should be permitted. I'm not a complete and total libertarian. For instance, I think allowing gay adults to marry should be the end of the marital contract's extension. Every American citizen should be able to marry one willing citizen.

We shouldn't, for instance, permit polygamy.

And marriage should always encompass adults and not children.

At some point, we have reached the end of marital tolerance. That's where we are now. This is it. We've reached the full and logical extension of the marital union. And guess what? That's okay! Eventually there needs to be an end to progressivism. That's called sanity.

And that's where embracing gay marriage brings us, to a dead end. Gay marriage is, to me, the logical end of marital tolerance. There's nothing else, no new battles on the marital front to fight. Anything else from this point forward takes you over the woke waterfall of absurdity, which I will examine in a chapter to come.

But first I'd like you to promise me that you'll teach your own kids the simple life goals I laid out above: graduate from high school, get married, get a job, and don't have kids until you're at least twenty-five. If everyone in the United States did this, we would eliminate poverty in this country.

That seems like a pretty good goal.

Even better, it doesn't require governmental involvement. It just requires individual responsibility and strong life choices.

Democrats are going to base much of their 2024 campaign on abortion and gay rights. They see these as the issues that motivate their voters, particularly suburban voters, and allow them to portray Republicans as extremists.

Republicans can't allow this to happen. As I said at the beginning of the chapter, sometimes you have to acknowledge the strengths of your opponent and limit their abilities to make plays as best you can.

If Republicans follow my advice above, they can flip the script and turn two losing issues into winners, further forcing Democrats to double down on their woke idiocy.

CHAPTER 9

DATA AND ANALYTICS ARE YOUR FRIENDS: USE THEM AGGRESSIVELY

In the past fifteen years many of the most successful teams have supplemented their playbook with advanced analytics. It turns out that sometimes the story that we see with our eyes isn't supported by the data from the minutes the players play. Whether it's on-base percentage (the foundational tenet praised in the book *Moneyball* for the Oakland A's success despite spending less money than other teams on players) and Wins Above Replacement Value in Major League Baseball, or plus/minus in basketball, many of these analytics terms have become commonplace for coaches, team executives, and fans.

In politics, all too often the narrative, especially the narrative set by social media, is based on anecdotal outliers. That is, an individual incident occurs and there's a rush to respond to that incident, which, as we discussed in our chapter on social media, often leads to a poor decision being made that may cause worse problems.

The data and analytics on crime tell a profoundly different story than the one advanced by Black Lives Matter and Democrats. Indeed, if Republicans use hard factual data to replace anecdotal attacks on police, then the war on law enforcement, cries to defund the police, and allegations of police racism will all vanish as legitimate arguments.

In sports, advanced data and analytics can often give you a substantial competitive advantage. The same is true in politics. Facts often destroy emotional, anecdote-driven policies. Especially in cases involving race and policing.

We just finished discussing abortion and gay marriage. Now let's dive into another easy subject without any pratfalls at all—minorities and policing. (Yes, you may need to pour yourself another drink.)

In May 2020, George Floyd was murdered by police in Minneapolis and the entire country fell apart amid months of Black Lives Matter protests.

As awful as the George Floyd video was, it represented an outlier when it comes to police and citizen interactions. That is, what happened to Floyd is not remotely reflective of typical police interactions with any white, black, Asian, or Hispanic person. Also, it should go without saying, but any police officer who commits any crime, especially a serious crime, should be prosecuted to the fullest extent of the law. Most police do not commit crimes, but those who do should not be above the law.

In the wake of Floyd's viral video, protests surged across the country and police were demonized. So demonized, in fact, that woke left-wing activists, most of them white, demanded the police be defunded. These left-wing activists wanted the money that had previously been spent by cities and states to pay police to be taken from the police budgets and spent elsewhere.

As a result of the Floyd incident, things were so bad for the perception of police that they pulled the long-running show *Cops* off television. It got so bad for police that the police officer on the popular children's television show *Paw Patrol* was challenged. I mean, you can't even make up this insanity. Before it was all over, "defund the police," which I believe is the single dumbest and most destructive political slogan of the twenty-first century, had put every single one of us in more danger. And it didn't take long for the results of the defund-the-police movement to arrive in our country.

Murder rates skyrocketed by 30 percent in 2020, according to FBI data, the highest increase on record in American history. They went up again in 2021 and in many places in 2022 as well, even though the number of murders dropped overall by a tiny amount in 2022. The overwhelming majority of these murder victims? Minorities in inner-city neighborhoods.

Yes, the tragic irony is that the Black Lives Matter protests actually led to far more black lives being lost. But not at the hands of police: at the hands of violent criminals. The data tells the story. From 2010 to 2019 there were an average of 6,927 black people murdered in the United States. In 2020 that number skyrocketed to 9,941 black murders. That means in one year the rate of black murders surged by 43 percent. And do you know who committed almost all of these murders? Black people.

You probably haven't seen this data anywhere because it points directly to the devastating impact of the Black Lives Matter movement on the black population. Prior to George Floyd's death, murder rates in 2020 were actually trailing the 2019 numbers, then they skyrocketed from his death forward, surging more in a single year than any other year in recorded FBI history. Sadly, this continues the trend noticed by scholars Roland Fryer and Tanaya Devi, who studied crime in the wake of viral police misconduct stories and found the result was a reduced police presence due to political pressures. Indeed, in cities like Baltimore and Chicago, police-civilian encounters plummeted by 90 percent after viral police misconduct stories. As police pull back, criminals move in, they found. The result? An average of 450 excess homicides per year in these cities. As the *Wall Street Journal* reported, that's twice the number of US military members who typically die each year; 12.6 times the annual loss of life due to school shootings; and, staggeringly, three times as many deaths as occurred by lynching from 1882 to 1901, the most deadly years for racial lynchings in US history.

The simple truth of the matter is this: no one protects more black lives from murder than police. Yet each time an issue of police misconduct occurs, far from making things better, the political furor that rolls in leads to more deaths, most of them black, than would have existed if the viral incident had never gone public in the first place. If black lives matter, then tragically these BLM protests actually lead to fewer black lives. Instead of making black people safer, they put more black lives in danger.

How did this happen? How did a movement like BLM, which purports to be directly focused on the sanctity and protection of black life, end up leading to more black lives lost in a single year, 2020, than in any decade of the twenty-first century? I'll tell you: because Democrats attacked police and policing, leaving our cities as killing fields. Turning police into objects of ridicule and disrespect created a massive increase in the murder rate. Notwithstanding the horrific George Floyd video, it turns out police were the solution, not the problem, when it comes to violent crime in our cities.

This is all too often what social media does: it destroys public institutions that are imperfect, but worthy of respect and continuing influence, and replaces them with something much worse. That's the argument Republicans should make more cogently and authoritatively: if something has endured for a substantial amount of time, that doesn't mean it should continue enduring forever, but it does suggest there's something of value to it, especially if there's nothing better to replace it with.

We can't just tear everything down in America and expect things to get better.

"Defund the police" wasn't just a dumb slogan. It was also nonsensical on its face. The fact that this slogan ever attained any power at all is a failure of American public debate. Did anyone seriously think that having fewer police on the streets would make our communities safer? It's completely illogical.

No one even bothered to answer basic questions on this issue. If you removed police from the cities, who would you call when danger arrived? Social workers? No one had any good answers to this question, but embarrassingly, most media and politicians didn't even ask it.

Why?

My own theory is because there was too much fear of being

branded racist. Heck, some people will call me racist for just sharing the above data on murders in America. How dare I point out who the overwhelming victims of increased murder in this country are?! My facts are racist, the woke will yell.

Plus, most of the loudest demands for defunding the police didn't come from minorities in inner-city neighborhoods—the data reflected most of these people want active police—it actually came from woke white people, many of whom are college educated and live in very safe neighborhoods. Indeed, the wokest, whitest big city in America, Portland, Oregon, suffered some of the most severe consequences of BLM protests.

Portland is so white and woke they even made a TV show about it, *Portlandia*, which satirized the left-wing worldview that predominates in the Pacific Northwest. Well, what has happened in Portland, a city filled with huge masses of white people, in the wake of the George Floyd protests?

Crime of all types has skyrocketed, but what I want to focus on in particular here is what's happened to murders in Portland. Focusing on murders makes sense because the data on murders is more reliable. People might report or not report burglaries, robberies, or assaults, but the dead body of a person who met a violent and untimely end is pretty concrete evidence of a murder.

For much of the twenty-first century, Portland was a quiet and safe place without much crime, especially murder. From 2000 to 2019 Portland averaged just 21 murders a year. Then the George Floyd protests began and, as we noted above, murder skyrocketed nationwide, increasing by 30 percent, the largest rate on record in history, from 2019 to 2020. Then it went up again in 2021 and stayed elevated in 2022 as well.

In 2021, Portland had 87 murders.

Eighty-seven!

After nearly a generation of averaging 21 murders, Portland saw a quadrupling of the overall rate by 2021. Why did that happen? Because the more woke a community becomes, the more it rejects policing and the more crime skyrockets.

This occurred especially in the Pacific Northwest, the woke white capital of America. Homicides surged in Portland, Seattle, and San Francisco at even higher rates than in the rest of the country. Woke white people, who suddenly decided police were evil, created massive increases in death, and many of those deaths, unfortunately, centered on black and brown communities in their cities.

This bears repeating: woke white people, the people who claim to care the most about racial injustice in this country, actually led to more black deaths than if they'd done nothing at all. The data is quite clear: there would be far more black people alive today if woke white people had done nothing at all.

What's particularly galling about the defund-the-police movement is how small the support for doing that actually is. According to a late winter of 2021 survey from Pew Research, just 15 percent of Americans want to decrease funding for police. Meanwhile, 47 percent believe that spending on police should *increase*, and the rest of the population believes funding should stay around the same. So 85 percent of Americans believe police funding should stay the same or increase, and three times as many people want to increase police funding as to defund.

It's not just that "defund the police" was a bad slogan with awful consequences; it's that the movement hijacked what the vast majority of the American public wanted. Each minority group, significantly, also favored spending the same or more money on police, including 77 percent of black, 84 percent of Hispanic, and 78 percent of Asian people. (Eighty-seven percent of white people, too.) In an era when it's hard to get Americans to agree on much of anything, the data clearly shows that more than three out of four of every racial group want police funding to stay the same or increase.

Here's a truth that receives minimal media attention: police are not racist. The data doesn't back up that accusation at all. Democrats have convinced much of the American public of this truth, but it's a falsehood.

The *Washington Post* aggressively tracks police shootings. Since 2015, in the wake of the Michael Brown incident in Ferguson, Missouri—remember, "hands up, don't shoot" was another lie; that didn't happen—they have attempted to catalog all police shootings that occur in our country. As I write this there are more than 7,500 people who have been shot and killed by police in the past seven years. Of this number, 3,183 were white, 1,678 were black, 1,127 were Hispanic, 256 were other, and 1,438 were of an unknown race.

So the race of people who were shot by police looks like this:

51% white
27% black
18% Hispanic
4% other

This means 73 percent of all people shot and killed by police in the past seven years were white, Hispanic, Asian, or of other races. Consider this data. Does it stun you that nearly three in four people shot and killed by police over the past seven years have been a race other than black? It stuns many, for sure.

In fact, I bet you've never even seen this data anywhere before.

Because the way the media covers these police shootings, you'd think cops were shooting only black people.

Now, let me be clear, I wish the police never had to shoot anyone, but of all the police shootings listed above, just 6 percent of them were of people who were "unarmed." That is, 94 percent of all people shot by police were armed with a weapon at the time of the shooting.

And of the small percentage of people who were unarmed and shot by police? The majority were still white!

Here are those numbers for you:

42% white

33% black

20% Hispanic

5% other

Significantly, we're talking about 450 people in seven years being shot and killed by police while unarmed, with 67 percent of those being shot and killed by police being white, Hispanic, Asian, or other.

Again, does this data surprise you?

I bet it does. In fact, I bet it shocks you.

The total number of unarmed individuals shot and killed by police is insanely low, an average of 57 people a year in a country of 330 million. (An average of 24 white, 18 black, 12 Hispanic, and 3 Asian or other races a year.) You are more likely to be killed by a bee, wasp, or hornet than you are to be unarmed and killed by police.

Now, remember, unarmed doesn't mean without danger; a person choking another person or reaching for an officer's weapon would, for instance, be considered unarmed. Certainly we all wish that none of these shootings ever occurred, that the police never needed to shoot anyone, but America is a violent place, made more violent, to be sure, by policies designed to defund the police and discredit the work they do to make us all safer.

Having seen all of this data, many of the woke will respond by saying, what about the per capita rate? Black people make up around 12 percent of the United States population and are being shot and killed at roughly twice the rate of their population. Isn't this discrepancy clear evidence of racism?

Well, let's analyze who actually interacts with police.

Women are half the population in this country. Yet they represent 4.5 percent of all people shot and killed by police in the past seven years. That is, 95.5 percent of police shootings involve men. Well, given that women only represent 4.5 percent of all police shootings yet represent half of the nation's population, how are men allowing this clear sexism to stand? Why are police so sexist against men?

Obviously, this is sarcasm.

I don't think anyone reading this book believes the difference in police shootings between men and women is based on sexism. Men are shot by police more often than women because men are more violent than women. The odds of your grandma being shot and killed by police are, quite honestly, nearly zero. (And that's not just because you killed her by refusing to wear your mask appropriately during Covid.)

Why?

Because old people aren't committing violent crimes very often! Almost no elderly people are shot and killed by police.

When you examine the data on, for instance, murders, which is the most violent of violent crime, you find that black people are actually less likely to be shot as a percentage of violent crime. (Black people represent 12 percent of the population and commit more than half of all murders, 93 percent of which are of people of their own race.) Contrary to the way race is covered in this country, almost all murders aren't across racial lines; people are almost always killed by someone of their own race. (Also contrary to the media narrative, white people are actually far more likely to be victims of black violence than black people are to be victims of white violence.)

If you're a woman reading this—hi, ladies—the person most likely to kill you is your husband or boyfriend. So if he's sleeping beside you while you read this book, if there's ever a Lifetime movie made about your life, it's probably going to be because you picked the wrong guy to marry or date. (Side note: Did you ever notice that women love movies about women being killed by their husbands? This, aside from all the Christmas movies, is like the entire Lifetime genre. So for the men reading this right now, every woman you've ever dated has, at one point or another, probably thought you would kill her. Which brings me to a fun wedding game you can play: Close your eyes and listen to the bridesmaid's speech at almost any wedding. Listen to how often the groom is described as madly pursuing his bride, how many times he had to ask her out, about the time he showed up unexpectedly with roses or bearing a gift, and what you realize is there's a really fine line between a restraining order and a marriage.)

The reason police shoot people isn't that police are racist, it's that they shoot people, on average, at rates nearly identical to those at which the races commit violent crimes.

Indeed, one reason the black shooting rate is actually lower than the violent crime rate is because police, especially white police, are terrified to shoot any black person, because they know they'll be judged more harshly in the media for that than for shooting any other race. A large Harvard study found that police were actually less likely to shoot black people than other races when adjustments for violent crime rates are made.

This brings us back to the larger context of violent crime in general. If black lives matter so much, why do they seem to matter only when they are taken by white police officers? If we eliminated every police shooting of black people in America today, 98 percent of black people would still be shot and killed. And almost all the time they're being shot by other black people. So why is it that we almost never hear about any shooting of black people unless a white police officer is involved?

Because, quite simply, the media doesn't care if they can't make shootings a racial issue.

Sadly, the recent police beating of Tyre Nichols is a good example of this. Five black Memphis police officers were on tape beating Nichols so severely that he later died. There was no justification for the police's initial stop of Nichols and their use of force was egregious. Personally, I found the footage of Nichols's beating far worse than the George Floyd footage. Yet there was virtually no rioting anywhere in the country, and within a week the story had completely disappeared. Imagine what the reaction would have been if Nichols had been beaten to death by five white cops.

Many parts of many different American cities would have likely burned down.

But why is that the case? If black lives truly matter, America should have been far more outraged by what happened to Nichols than what happened to Floyd, or at least similarly outraged. Yet the nation wasn't. There are no statues of Tyre Nichols anywhere. Why?

Because black cops being the accused murderers took away the racial victimization angle of the story. Sadly, the life of a black man seems to matter only when a white man is involved in taking it.

It's not actually Black Lives Matter. It's Black Lives Matter (When White People Are Involved in Killing Them).

Let's return to the George Floyd incident and what occurred in Minneapolis in the wake of his death. Surely, of all places, Minneapolis has been able to find some positive change in the wake of Floyd's death, right?

Wrong.

There's almost no media still covering violent crime in Minneapolis, the city where Floyd was killed. As soon as the protest ended, most of the media vanished. That's why you probably haven't read any of the data I'm about to share with you.

In 2019, the year before George Floyd died, Minneapolis had 54 murders. By 2021, as the full effect of the attack on police became apparent, murders soared to 101, nearly a doubling of murders from just two years earlier and, significantly, an all-time high for murders in the city. The lesson here is crystal clear: as the national media attention vanished and the residents of Minneapolis returned to their new normal, violent crime skyrocketed, murders hit an all-time high, and almost no one cared in the national media.

In fact, I bet most of you reading this right now had no idea how much violent crime in Minneapolis surged after Floyd's death and the BLM protests began to recede. Left behind were the real residents of the city, people who now felt far less safe in the neighborhoods they called home, people who were frequently begging for police to help them. Only there were, increasingly, no police there to help.

The war on police had very real consequences beyond just an increase in violent crime, which was bad enough. In fact, many Minneapolis police simply retired or left the force. Indeed, in June 2020, right as the George Floyd protests exploded in their city, there were 890 police at work in Minneapolis. By June 2022 there were only 626 police officers left on the force, hundreds of police having quit, retired, or relocated. Things were so bad that the Minnesota Supreme Court ordered the city to explain why they didn't have sufficient police to do the job of protecting their citizenry.

But think about it: Would you want to work as a police officer in Minneapolis right now? Most of you probably wouldn't. If you could retire or find another job, you probably would. And almost no one would voluntarily choose to go to work in Minneapolis as a police officer, when the police force is considered the enemy by a substantial portion of the city's residents and all the media.

Portland and Minneapolis are two examples of cities where

murders surged, but they weren't alone. It was all of our nation's biggest cities. Between 2019 and 2021, murders in San Francisco soared by 37 percent, in New York City by 53 percent, in Philadelphia by 58 percent, and in Chicago by 60 percent. This is a nationwide problem, from coast to coast. And it's not getting better, because police are still being demonized.

As I stated at the beginning of this chapter, we certainly need to prosecute police who break the law, but we also need to realize that demonizing police has the very real consequence of leading to thousands of more homicides, to turning our cities into killing fields.

All of the data that I've shared with you here is readily accessible. None of it is hidden. It's public for all to see. So why are so few Republicans willing to share this data and have real conversations about its consequences? I'll tell you: because many Republicans have bought into the left-wing idea that sharing information like this is racist.

That's because many white people, Democrat and Republican alike, fear being called racist more than they're willing to share the truth. And to some degree, that makes sense. It would be far better for my career for me to get multiple DUIs than it would be for me to utter a racial slur. Think about the absurdity of the world we've created: it would be better for most white people to commit multiple DUIs than speak aloud forbidden words (words that can, of course, be used in popular rap songs with impunity, but that's an entirely different discussion).

We can't solve problems without sharing facts—sometimes facts that might even make people uncomfortable—in an effort to address our underlying issues. We know what solves issues of crime. It's actually quite simple. Put more police on the streets in high-crime areas and when the police arrest bad guys, put them behind bars for substantial amounts of time.

This is what we did in the 1990s, when cities like New York, rapidly followed by others, decided to address violent crime and make our cities safe again. They put more police on the streets, arrested more bad guys, and put them behind bars, and crime fell all over our country. Then what happened? Crime got so low in many places that left-wing activists started to argue that police and our criminal justice system were racist.

So political leaders got squeamish, soft-on-crime prosecutors supported by George Soros were hired all over the country, and suddenly crime began to increase again. What we know to be true is this: being concerned that you're being too hard on criminals is a luxury of a low-crime environment.

We don't live in a low-crime environment any longer.

A Republican candidate who wants to win a landslide victory in 2024 needs to advocate for hiring more police and putting more criminals behind bars for longer sentences. That candidate also needs to be willing to have uncomfortable conversations about who commits crimes and what that will mean for who is being arrested and prosecuted for those crimes.

Crime is not committed equally by all races. Black people are far more likely to commit violent crimes than, for instance, Asian people are. It's not racist to point out these facts. Indeed, it's only by doing so that issues of crime in our country can be addressed.

The reason is that crime doesn't occur evenly in our cities, either. A relatively tiny subset of neighborhoods account for a huge number of our citywide crimes. In order to reduce those crimes we have to make criminals uncomfortable. That requires bringing back some police tactics—such as stop, frisk, and question—that left-wing activists attacked as racist.

I've got a crazy idea. You know what I think is racist? Letting thousands of innocent black people be murdered every year instead of solving our national crime issue and making all of our citizens safer.

A Republican candidate has to be willing to 100 percent support police and the tactics they embrace to bring down crime. Now, again, it doesn't mean that every police officer is perfect or that no police officers should ever be charged with crimes, but it does mean that in order to have safer streets we have to hire more officers and elect prosecutors who insist on stiff penalties and locking up repeat offenders.

A chilling study came out of Baltimore recently that found that 90 percent of known murderers—remember, most murder cases aren't solved in big cities—were committed by people who shouldn't have been on the streets, based on their past criminal history. That is, if prosecutors had done their jobs and actually charged these violent criminals and sought the sentences they deserved, their victims would still be alive.

During the late summer of 2022, another awful thing happened in my home state of Tennessee, just down the road in Memphis, seven months before Tyre Nichols was beaten to death. A mother of young children, Eliza Fletcher, was out for an early morning jog when she was raped and murdered by a felon who had been released early on parole. Eliza Fletcher is dead today, and her kids don't have a mom, because my home state let a violent felon out of jail early and he did what violent felons often do: attack an innocent victim.

It's long past time for Republicans to stand up and be counted on this issue. We also have to shoot down the Democrat argument that there are too many nonviolent convictions. Do you know why many people are in jail for nonviolent offenses? Because they pled down their violent offenses to a lesser charge!

We shouldn't be defunding the police. We should be funding them at higher levels, period.

You know who once got this right?

Joe Biden.

As a senator he supported the 1994 crime bill, which helped ensure our nation's crime rate plummeted through the 1990s and into the early twenty-first century. But in the 2020 presidential campaign, Biden repudiated that vote, the one thing he'd gotten most right in his political career, because now he endorsed the Democrat idea that our nation was putting too many criminals behind bars.

The number one job of any politician is to protect the lives of the people in his community, whether black, white, Asian, or Hispanic. Right now Democrats are utterly failing at this responsibility. The right Republican candidate, through logic, analytics, and data, can make the persuasive case that justice for all requires more police and more criminals behind bars.

It's an argument we must make and an argument we must win.

All lives depend on it.

CHAPTER 10

KEEP RUNNING THE PLAY THAT YOUR OPPONENT CAN'T DEFEND

One of the most important lessons of any playbook is this: you select the plays that are most likely to work against an opponent, and when you find one that the other team can't defend, you keep running it over and over again until they prove they can stop it. The best play of all is one that, due to the inferior abilities of your opponent, they simply can't defend. This rarely happens in highly competitive athletic endeavors. But it's going to happen in politics in 2024. Democrats are so far left-wing on issues related to transgenderism that they have no ability to defend their positions to more than three-fourths of the American public.

So Republicans have to absolutely hammer this issue day and night between now and the 2024 election.

As I wrote earlier, I entered the political arena through sports. Many people ask me how that happened, and the answer is quite simple: sports became so infected by politics they became virtually indistinguishable. That's really the subject of my last book, *Republicans Buy Sneakers Too*, which I'd humbly encourage you all to go read because it's the most significant sports book of the twenty-first century.

Again, I say humbly.

Much of that book looks at the wokeification of American sports and how that infestation of wokeness destroyed sports from the inside. There are two specific examples of this destruction of sports I'd like to discuss here because I believe they are so significant: the rise of transgender athletes in women's sports and the NBA's charade of wokeness, which has destroyed its underlying brand.

Let's start with the rise of transgender athletes.

In the spring of 2022, a former University of Pennsylvania men's collegiate swimmer named Will Thomas officially transitioned into a women's swimmer named Lia Thomas. Prior to his transition, Will Thomas was six feet, four inches tall and had spent his entire life training as a swimmer. He was, at best, a mediocre college swimmer in the men's division. But then he decided to become a woman, and Lia Thomas debuted on the Penn women's swimming team in 2022.

Almost immediately Lia Thomas was one of the best women's swimmers in the country, setting Ivy League records and dominating the season en route to capturing the 500-meter women's NCAA title. By the end of "her" career, Lia was nominated as the NCAA Woman of the Year by the University of Pennsylvania.

There is an awful lot of discussion about white privilege in the country today, but crazily, no one pointed out that Will Thomas is actually the very definition of white privilege. Here you have a white male athlete attending an Ivy League school who decided to become a woman and didn't just become a woman—he became one of the best women swimmers and was nominated as a woman of the year. You want to talk about privilege? This dude was so privileged he became one of the greatest women swimmers of all time in just a couple of years.

Too bad for all those little girls who have been training all their lives, waking up at dawn since elementary school to work on their craft. You're nothing compared to a dude who decided he was a girl after he'd already gotten to college and participated on the men's swimming team.

Outkick.com, the sports site I run, featured stories during the winter and spring about Thomas's dominance. Included in those stories were anonymous interviews with women on the Penn team who were upset about a biological man being allowed to compete as a woman athlete. Why did the women feel the need to be anonymous? Because they feared if they spoke out against Lia's membership on the team they'd be unable to get into grad school or get jobs. These women were so afraid to speak out because they feared being labeled transphobic.

Things were so bad that one of the Penn women's swimmers even worried about the future of all women's sports on her future children's behalf, telling Outkick, "When I have kids, I kinda hope they're all boys because if I have any girls that want to play sports in college, good luck. Their opponents are all going to be biological men saying they're women. Right now we have one, but what if we had three on the team? There'd be three less girls competing."

Biological men should not be competing against women in women's sports.

Period.

This should be a clear and straightforward line adopted by any Republican who wants to win a landslide election in 2024.

Overwhelming majorities of men, women, gay, straight, black, white, Asian, and Hispanic sports fans agree that this shouldn't be permitted. It's not transphobic to require men and women to compete against members of their biological sex.

Men are bigger, faster, and stronger than women. This is a biological reality. It's beyond insane to allow a man to identify as a woman and begin to compete with women in any sport.

What we're really talking about here isn't transphobia; it's simple fairness in competition.

Let's step back from the trans issue and just consider fairness in sports in general. We already adjust competitions based on age, weight, sex, and even size of schools. A sixteen-year-old doesn't get to play against twelve-year-olds in Little League baseball. Why not? Because the sixteen-year-old would crush the twelve-year-old. We don't allow someone to be "trans age." If I suddenly identified as a twelve-year-old boy, I would be the MVP of the Little League World Series. I would smoke those kids. I'd hit a homer almost every time I came up to bat. I'd be the greatest twelve-year-old Little League player of all time.

At forty-three years old.

It would be ridiculous and no one would allow it to happen because it would defeat the entire purpose of having age limits.

Similarly, Mike Tyson is over fifty years old now. He's the

former heavyweight champion of the world, but if you put him in a ring with flyweights today, that is, boxers who weigh 112 pounds, he'd probably be able to win the title. If you'd let Tyson in his prime fight against boxers who weighed far less than him, he probably would have killed someone in the ring.

That's why we have weight classes in boxing and UFC.

It goes on and on. We have different classifications of schools based on the number of students who attend them. The rationale? A high school that has 4,000 students is probably way better at sports than one that has 500. They just have way more kids to pick from for their teams.

I lay out all of these rationales, none of which are considered remotely controversial, to make it clear that we set up sports leagues to try to ensure fairness of competition. Heck, the reason we have women's sports at all is that if we just had a unisex league, almost no women would be able to play sports—they wouldn't be able to beat out men to be on the team. If you doubt me, look at what happened to the US women's soccer team a few years ago. Those women practiced for the World Cup by scrimmaging against a top fifteen-and-under boys' team from Dallas. These weren't the top boys age fifteen and under in the country, just the top boys fifteen and under in Dallas. The boys beat the US women's team 5–2.

Let me repeat: the best women's soccer team in the world got smoked by a team of boys fifteen and under.

And that's not unique.

Sha'Carri Richardson is the fastest woman in the world right now. But every high school boy was faster than her in every racing division in the Texas high school state championships. Again, we're not talking about one boy in the nation: every high school boy sprinter state champion, in every classification in Texas, from small schools to big schools, was faster than the fastest woman on the planet right now.

I'm not trying to denigrate female performance. I'm just trying to make it as clear as possible that men are bigger, stronger, and faster than women. Indeed, it's not just grown men; it's often boys, who are still competing in high school. Remember, we're not talking about all transgender athletes here, either, just men who identify as women. Most women who identify as men can't make the men's sports teams because they aren't bigger, stronger, and faster than their male counterparts, hence competitive balance isn't impacted at all.

But when you allow a biological man to identify as a woman and become a women's champion, you are destroying the fabric of women's sports. The anonymous Penn women's swimming team member above is not wrong; eventually men identifying as women will become the greatest "women's" athletes of all time. You don't erase all the advantages of male puberty and testosterone by taking estrogen for a few months. Will/Lia Thomas was still the same height with the same hand and feet sizes, whether he was identifying as a man or a woman. That's why Will Thomas was a mediocre male college swimmer and a dominant women's college swimmer. Given the increasing prevalence of men identifying as women, this is a real issue that's going to become commonplace in every state and every sport at some point in the next five to ten years.

So where are the feminists? Shouldn't they be standing up for women athletes, defending Title IX and the ability of women to compete in their own sport against other women? You'd expect to hear from them. But you won't. Because they're mostly silent. There is so much fear in our country right now that even saying something like "Women shouldn't be competing against biological men" is considered extremely transphobic by left-wing communities.

The Biden administration even, and I can't believe this is real, rewrote Title IX to ensure that men who identify as women retain the right to compete in athletic competitions as women. Yes, you heard that right: Title IX now is so broadly defined that according to the Biden administration it protects the rights of men to identify as women and compete to win women's championships!

Heck, the trans agenda is in fact so ascendant right now that left-wingers are legitimately arguing—and this isn't even an exaggeration—that men can get pregnant and that sometimes doctors get the sex of babies wrong when they are born. They're even referring to pregnant women now as "pregnant people" to avoid offending transgender people. (Even when women decide to become men, they retain their uterus. So "men" who are still biological women can get pregnant under this ascendant dogma. As for doctors getting the sex of babies wrong, many trans activists argue that doctors and nurses, who determine sex by looking at the genitals of babies, misidentify them. I mean, this is truly antiscience lunacy. Biology is real. But for many trans activists, that's not the case.) These are actual trans talking points. Fortunately these insane ideas are completely rejected by overwhelming numbers of white, black, Asian, and Hispanic people in the United States.

According to a recent *Washington Post* poll, just 28 percent of

Americans believe men identifying as women should be able to compete in women's college or pro sports. Just as with defunding the police, a small minority of the public is driving this narrative. I would argue 28 percent is even too high because many people truly don't understand the competitive imbalance that biological men who identify as women create in sports.

So many Americans of all backgrounds reject the idea that men shouldn't be able to identify as women and compete in women's sports that even the woke NBA is avoiding this battleground. Back in 2017, the NBA pulled its all-star game from Charlotte, North Carolina, over a transgender bathroom bill in North Carolina that would have required transgender people to use the bathrooms of the gender on their birth certificates. It was a horribly hypocritical move by the league because the NBA plays games in China and even the Middle East, in the United Arab Emirates, where it's still permissible to punish homosexuality with a beheading. But the NBA moved its all-star game and all the usual woke suspects applauded the hypocritical move.

But the NBA All-Star Game in 2023 was played in Utah, where a recent bill passed by the state legislature requires high school athletes to compete against the gender on their birth certificates. That is, a Lia Thomas situation is specifically prohibited by state law in Utah. So what's the NBA's position on this law? Here's what NBA commissioner Adam Silver said: "Our view, today, is that making threats that we're going to move the All-Star Game would not be constructive." Asked specifically about why the league would move the game from Charlotte and not Salt Lake City, Silver said, "We're going to have to find a way to work in that environment and create an inclusive environment for our game, rather than take the position that we have, somehow, an independent ability to change the minds of the voters of Utah in this."

I wonder what changed here in the space of six years?

I'll tell you: the polling.

Even the incredibly woke NBA is aware that boys competing against girls is an impossible public policy position to take up. Sports fans of all political persuasions reject this absurdity. So much so that even the woke NBA won't fight this battle.

(Utah also passed a bill forbidding minors from receiving any medical treatments to alter their genders. The NBA stayed silent on this issue as well, proving that in the space of six years an awful lot had changed.)

The NBA's silence in Utah is also, I believe, a strong argument that fans standing up against NBA wokeism run amok is beginning to have a substantial impact on the choices the league is making.

This is where the 2024 landslide argument comes in: if a grown man or woman decides they want to change their gender, they should be able to do so. I believe grown adults should have the freedom to make decisions that, at least theoretically, make them happier. But the idea that kids younger than eighteen should be having surgeries to change their sex, having their breasts removed—that's child abuse. You can't vote until you're eighteen, we don't even let kids younger than twenty-one buy a beer, and in many places you can't rent a car until you're twenty-five, but we're letting fourteen- or sixteen-year-olds decide to identify as a different sex and in some places even compete against the opposite sex? That's flat-out wrong.

Heck, we don't let kids get tattoos in most states if they are under eighteen years old. Indeed, we will even hold parents responsible if their kids make the decision to get tattoos in some states. But we let them chop their breasts off at fourteen or fifteen? This is madness.

It's staggering to me that more Republicans aren't arguing against these fundamentally indefensible positions. As I laid out above, it's not transphobic to insist on fair sporting competitions. Even the woke NBA won't argue against it. The NBA is so woke they removed the word *owners* from league bylaws to refer to the people who own the teams and instead called them *governors* because some idiots in sports considered it racially insensitive for majority-white team owners to be referred to owning teams made up of majority-black players because it harked back to the days of slavery.

Yes, the NBA really is that dumb and woke.

This brings me back to the feminists and the women's sports advocates—they're mostly silent on the trans issue not because they agree with men crushing women in women's sports, but because their identity politics hierarchies are upset by this issue. See, Democrats believe in the oppression Olympics, the idea that the most oppressed person should win an argument, not the person who has the better side.

In a situation like this, they're in a really difficult spot. Who is the victim, the biological woman who isn't allowed to compete against other women and loses a sporting event to a man identifying as a woman, or the trans person who isn't able to compete? They have no idea how to pick a winner in this situation, so they pretend that the issue doesn't exist.

It's the same reason Democrats have incoherent rules on race and sex. Remember Rachel Dolezal, the white woman who pretended to be black to join the NAACP? Remember the outrage that ensued when Dolezal identified as black even though she was white? That was unacceptable cultural appropriation. But isn't it far easier to change your race than to change your gender?

Do you think you have more in common with members of your same gender or your same race? For me, this isn't even a difficult question. I believe I have far more in common with men of any race than I do with white women. And as we saw above, identifying with a race is far easier than changing your gender since race is very often cultural, whereas gender is biological. You can often change the race you identify as without anyone even knowing.

Indeed, with all the DNA test kits out there these days, many people are even finding out they have identified as a race different than the one they had been for most of their lives. Just look at Senator Elizabeth "Pocahontas" Warren, who is 1/1024th Native American according to her own DNA results. Yet this didn't stop her from identifying as a Native American for the purpose of getting minority teaching jobs her entire life. Or contributing cooking recipes, which she stole from another person, to a Native American cookbook called, wait for it, *Pow Wow Chow*.

There are even white guys, like "racial activist" Shaun King, who claim to be black despite zero evidence they are actually black. I even offered $50,000 to King's charity if he would take a DNA test and that test showed him to be more than 10 percent black. Not surprisingly, King refused my charitable offer. Here I am, just trying to make the world a better place and bring the races together, and King won't even accept my offer. From one white guy to another white guy, I reiterate my $50,000 offer. With the caveat that I'll get to donate the money myself, since King has previously been accused of mishandling charitable donations.

Notwithstanding the fact that people regularly lie about their race, when someone is caught doing that, that is, pretending to be in a racial group they aren't a member of, it's considered to be incredibly racist. People are furious. That got me wondering: If it's racist to change your race, why isn't it sexist to change your sex?

After all, it's far easier to change your race. As we noted above, people have changed their race and been undiscovered for a long time. It doesn't even require any real work at all to change your race; it's not like you need surgery to do so. Yet that's considered to be completely unacceptable by left-wingers.

So why don't we apply the same rules to people who change their gender? By the way, I really don't care that much what race or sex someone identifies as, but if one is societally impermissible—changing your race—and the other is considered brave—changing your gender—why do we have the difference in treatment? Shouldn't it be just as unacceptable to change your sex as it is to change your race?

Because let's be clear: biology is real. No one who "changes" their sex is actually doing so. Men can't get pregnant and women can't make babies by producing sperm. That's impossible. The fact that the "party of science" has adopted this fiction is pure, unadulterated madness. Again, if you're an adult, you should have the freedom to live life as you see fit. The Republican Party should be the party of individual freedom. If you're an adult and you want to pretend to be a man or pretend to be a woman and that makes you happier, go for it, but that should also mean people can pretend to be whatever race they want to be, too.

You should even be able to change your race and gender on a daily basis.

Tomorrow I might want to wake up and be an Asian woman. The next day I might want to be a Hispanic man. If we're all just going to adopt the fiction that your gender is whatever you want it to be, why can't we embrace the same fiction on race and just make every day Halloween?

The fact that we've reached the point where being transgender is considered something that many kids aspire to, or that, God forbid, we're allowing kids to have surgery to cut their genitals off, is child abuse. We don't let kids buy a beer until twenty-one, but we let them cut their genitals off at fourteen? No one with a functional brain supports this.

Recent polling from the Trafalgar Group showed 78.7 percent of voters believe minors should have to wait to be adults to have sex change procedures. That included 84.6 percent of independent voters and even 53.2 percent of Democrats.

That's why it's the reasonable, rational argument that Republicans should make. Adults can do whatever makes them happy, but operating on kids is child abuse. So is giving them puberty blockers to prevent adolescence. And while we're on this subject, you don't get to pick your pronouns any more than you get to pick your adjectives. I don't get to demand that all of you refer to me as "ridiculously handsome" and "brilliant without parallel" every time you mention me in public. That's despite the fact that both of these things are objectively true. I am the most handsome and brilliant person I've ever known.

In my own mind, at least.

They is a plural that has been used for eons to denote more than one person. It isn't the middle ground between boys and girls. No, I will not let you tell me which pronouns to use for you. I'll look at the way you're dressed and make my best guess.

While Democrats want to pretend this issue isn't significant, I think they're wrong. It's completely indicative of where we are headed. You can't even rely on this transgender issue being solved in the world of sports because, crazily, sports has gone so far into the woke era that almost no one in sports media, except for me and the site I run, Outkick, will hardly even discuss an issue like this. Extreme wokeness, like this transgender issue, has infected all of our sports culture.

The NBA, in fact, provides a perfect distillation of what wokeness can do to an otherwise strong business with great mass appeal. Because wokeness, ultimately, destroys everything it touches.

THE NBA GOES FOR WOKE

I understand many of you may not pay much attention to sports. But sports is an important window into modern society and the NBA offers a cautionary tale on what happens when woke politics infests a sport.

The underlying business collapses.

Even if you're not a sports fan, you probably remember the Michael Jordan era of the NBA. The NBA has never been more popular than in 1998, when the Jordan-led Bulls played against the Utah Jazz in the NBA Finals. That year the Bulls, who would win their sixth title in eight years, played a six-game championship series against the Jazz. Game six of the NBA Finals had 35.89 million viewers. It was then, and remains today, the most-watched basketball game in American history. Indeed, the entire Bulls-Jazz series was wildly popular, averaging 29.04 million viewers for each game.

This was the high-water mark for the NBA in American life. That year, 1998, the NBA was closer to the NFL in total viewership than it would ever be. The 1998 Super Bowl would have 90 million viewers and the 1999 Super Bowl, played eight months after the Jordan NBA Finals, would have 83.72 million viewers. So the top-rated game of the 1998 NBA Finals was just 47.8 million viewers behind the 1999 Super Bowl.

It's the closest the two leagues would ever be in viewership.

By 2015 the NFL would have 114.4 million viewers for its Super Bowl, the highest ever. That same year the NBA would average 19.9 million viewers for its six-game NBA Finals, representing a nearly 95 million difference in viewership.

It was going to get worse from there.

The Jordan-era NBA represented a full embrace of American exceptionalism. The NBA of the 1990s wanted everyone— white, black, Asian, and Hispanic, Democrat or Republican, gay or straight—to consume its product. Your background didn't matter; the NBA wanted you inside its sporting tent. This was perfectly epitomized by one of the most famous statements of the era. When Jordan was asked why he wasn't more outspoken politically he said, "Republicans buy sneakers too." (This was the title of my fabulous last book, by the way, which I'd encourage you to go buy and read if you haven't already.)

And Republicans did buy his sneakers.

Jordan, despite being retired for nearly two decades, still outsells all current NBA player's sneakers combined.

Combined!

Why?

Because Americans want sports to be about something other than politics. They want to embrace the sporting meritocracy, elite athletes, no matter their background. Nike's business thrived in the Jordan era. How much so? If you had bought $10,000 in Nike stock on the day the Air Jordan sneaker was introduced and just held it to the present day, you'd now have $15 million in Nike stock!

The NBA rode this same rate of return, but then an incredibly strange thing happened as Jordan and older NBA players began to retire, including the stalwart superstars of the 1980s, 1990s, and early 2000s: Charles Barkley, Larry Bird, Patrick Ewing, Magic Johnson, Reggie Miller, John Stockton, and Karl Malone. The Kobe Bryant era, which to a large degree was a continuation of the Jordan era, was led disastrously astray by LeBron James during his era as the league's best player. LeBron, recognizing he would never be Jordan on the court, decided to become stridently left-wing and massively political. The drift of the league into politics picked up steam with the rise of social media in the 2010s but has accelerated in recent years, with all teams, for instance, refusing to visit the White House during Donald Trump's presidency. This culminated in the 2020 season, played inside a "bubble" in Orlando, Florida, lest some superhealthy player get Covid.

The NBA, in the wake of George Floyd, emblazoned its court with BLACK LIVES MATTER right at the center and instead of the players having their names on the back of their jersey, they put political slogans on everyone instead. Yes, this really happened. Among the slogans on the backs of these NBA jerseys: "Black Lives Matter," "Say Their Names," "Vote," "I Can't Breathe," "Say Her Name," "Anti-Racist," "I Am a Man," "How Many More," "Listen to Us," "Ally," "Power to the People," and "Justice Now." It was all completely insane.

Even now I can't believe this all happened.

Even crazier than this, NBA players refused to take the court and play playoff games after Jacob Blake was shot by police in Kenosha, Wisconsin. Blake, who had been armed with a knife and refused to drop it, was threatening a woman who had accused him of rape and that woman had called police, who were responding to protect her. Not that it should matter, but the woman who called asking them for help was a black woman. So NBA players refused to play their playoff games that year because a white police officer shot a black man who was threatening a black woman.

Even crazier?

The WNBA took it a step further and all posed on the court in T-shirts with Blake's name written on the shirts.

Yes, a league made up of a majority of black women all wore the name of a man accused of sexually assaulting a black woman.

Again, all of this really happened.

And it wasn't just the players. It was the far-left-wing media covering the teams, too.

When Missouri senator Josh Hawley sent a letter to the NBA asking them to explain why they refused to condemn China's genocidal acts in their country despite ridiculing American interests at every turn, one of ESPN's highest-paid reporters,

Adrian Wojnarowski, who had been added to the email as well, immediately responded to the senator's letter by emailing back, "Fuck you."

This is emblematic of sports media's cheerleading for the NBA's embrace of woke, far-left politics, which has clearly alienated a large portion of their audience. These media refuse to acknowledge the facts and data that I'm about to share with you. What do you think happened when the NBA went superwoke, turning its sports into a political commercial for left-wing interests in 2020?

NBA ratings tanked to a level they'd never fallen to before.

Get woke, go broke, indeed.

The 2020 season featured the least-watched NBA Finals game on record, with just 5.9 million viewers. The average NBA Finals game that year, which featured the Los Angeles Lakers, one of the most popular teams in NBA history, and LeBron James, the most popular player in the league, had just 7.5 million viewers.

So in the space of twenty-two years the NBA had gone from an average audience of 29 million viewers per NBA Finals game in 1998 during the Jordan era to an average of just 7.5 million viewers. Nearly 75 percent of the NBA's TV audience had just flat-out vanished. And not only that: the audience wasn't just smaller, there were actually 50 million more people in America in 2020 than were in the country in 1998. So the NBA's viewership hadn't just tanked; it had done so despite the fact that there were far more people in the potential market to watch.

The woke sports media will argue this wasn't because of politics and they'll argue that television ratings overall are down. But, again, let's compare it with the NFL. It's not like, by the way, the NFL wasn't political, too; it's just that the NFL wasn't anywhere near as political as the NBA.

The NFL's Super Bowl viewership at the end of the 2020 season? 91.6 million. (That was actually lower, too, than the 100 million Super Bowl viewers at the end of the 2019 season and the 99 million at the end of the 2022 season. This suggests that some viewers also tuned out of the NFL over political reasons.)

But even at 91.6 million, the NFL's viewership for the 2020 Super Bowl was higher than the 90 million who watched the 1998 Super Bowl. So the NFL, even in the worst year for Super Bowl viewership in nearly twenty years, still had more viewers in 2020 than they had in 1998. (One bit of data here: the Super Bowl is played in early February the year after the season. So I'm using the season year as opposed to the Super Bowl year.)

If everyone was simply abandoning sports, why hasn't the NFL's Super Bowl viewership also tanked over the past twenty-two years like the NBA Finals viewership has? And if 2020 was such an aberration for the NBA, why was the 2021 and 2022 viewership also a disaster for the NBA Finals? Because the woker you get, the more broke you go. And it's not just the NBA Finals: the 2023 NBA All-Star Game had just 4.59 million viewers, the lowest total viewership in league history. That game, as we mentioned above, was played in Salt Lake City. Salt Lake City last hosted the NBA All-Star Game in 1993. Do you know how many people watched that game? 22.9 million. So in the space of thirty years the NBA lost 85 percent of its all-star game viewership.

What's even more remarkable is that basketball itself has not seen plummeting ratings. In fact, the women's NCAA tournament championship game between LSU and Iowa actually had 9.9 million viewers in 2023, the highest viewership in women's basketball history, and more than the average NBA Finals game in 2020 and 2021. Men's NCAA tournament viewership also rose to near-record highs in the early rounds of 2023. It turns out that people love basketball—they just hate woke basketball.

Why am I using the NBA as an example here? Because sports provides perfect data showing that Americans of all stripes and persuasions hate woke politics so much that they will even change their viewing patterns for something they otherwise enjoy, sports, if something they like embraces woke politics.

Sports, for the right Republican candidate in 2024, is actually a perfect distillation of how radical modern-day Democrat policies are. Democrats believe that biological men should be able to compete against women in women's sports—becoming in some cases the all-time record holders and being hailed as women of the year—and that sports leagues should have slogans supporting woke politics on the backs of their jerseys.

This is a radical proposition, something that the vast majority of the American population overwhelmingly rejects, as we see by the objective data on TV ratings. That is why it's a perfect avenue for Republicans to embrace, a clear example of how a universal subject, sports, can stand as a test case for how to produce a landslide in 2024.

Democrats are completely out of touch with the general public on these issues, and the lesson in sports is applicable directly here: when your opponent can't defend a play, keep running it over and over again until either they stop it or you win a decisive victory. Here the Democrats can't defend their position because that requires they abandon identity politics, so Republicans have to just keep hammering this issue.

If Republicans deliver on this, they can make woke politics the anvil that has already sunk the NBA and they can do to the Democrats what the American sports fan has already done to the NBA—abandon it completely.

CHAPTER 11

HOLD LOSERS ACCOUNTABLE

If your playbook and your coaching sucks, you get fired. The performance of your team in games has consequences. Yet, remarkably, we've held our football coaches to a higher standard of performance than our politicians. When it comes to Covid almost no Democrat politician has lost his or her job despite the worst decision-making we've seen in any of our lives. That has to change. There must be a Covid policy reckoning in 2024.

On April 6, 2020, my forty-first birthday, the doorbell rang at my house.

We were in the middle of the Covid lockdowns all over the country and it was relatively rare that someone would be ringing my doorbell. My kids were out of school, climbing up and down the walls, driving my wife and me crazy, when I opened the door and saw a woman standing there holding a big box full of cupcakes.

As much as I appreciated cupcakes—seriously, who hates

cupcakes?—I was a bit surprised that with all the businesses currently forced to close, I was getting them delivered to my door for
my birthday.

"How are you guys still delivering cupcakes?" I asked.

"We're an essential business," said the cupcake delivery girl.

I didn't explode on her, but as soon as I shut the door, my rant
began. "Cupcakes are an essential business—cupcakes!" I ranted
to my wife as I carried the cupcakes back inside. "Our schools
can't be open and no gym in the entire state can be open, but
cupcakes can be delivered to our house and the cupcake store is
still open?!"

That same day, there was crime scene tape strung up around
my neighborhood playground to keep kids from playing on the
jungle gym or the swings. Rims were taken off outdoor basketball
hoops all over the country, paddleboarders with no one near them
were being arrested in California, beaches and public parks were
closed. You couldn't even go on a hiking trail in many parts of the
country.

There had been no sports for weeks, but I was still doing my
morning radio show for three hours every day. The nation was in
turmoil, many were terrified, and I was furious that lockdowns
were taking place anywhere. What's more, I was facing a big decision with Outkick: while everyone else was firing employees, I
was convinced it was the perfect time to expand my online site.

Yes, we hired a bunch of new employees at a media business
while everyone else was firing people.

I've always said I believe in creative freedom for Outkick employees, but I was so fired up, I put in place the only litmus test

I've ever asked of any of my employees. "You can believe in anything," I said, "except that it's not safe to play sports."

With virtually no one else in American sports media's support, certainly not anyone with a large national audience, I turned my radio show and my Outkick website into an unrequited force in favor of opening schools back up, playing sports, and returning our country to normalcy. For three hours every morning, even as the nation was in the grip of Covid lockdowns, we did a sports talk radio show with no actual sports to talk about.

And something crazy happened—our audience skyrocketed.

In March, April, and on into May, still no sports were being played, yet I was fighting as hard as I could for a return to normalcy. While virtually every other sports radio host took time off work, I promised my audience that I wouldn't take a day off until sports returned.

All day long every day, I obsessively studied data on Covid, and each morning I told my audience something they weren't hearing anywhere else—it was safe to play sports and put our kids back in schools.

Furious over lockdowns continuing, we loaded up our family and drove down to Florida to spend the month of May at the beach. I could do my radio show just as easily from the Florida Gulf Coast and I figured, when would we ever have a full month to spend at the beach without the kids having school or sports activities?

On one of our first days at the beach, which Governor Ron DeSantis had mercifully reopened, a Florida lawyer, who would run as a Democrat for Florida attorney general and get smoked in the 2022 election, dressed as the Grim Reaper, replete with a scythe, and stalked the sand, telling all of us we were going to die of Covid for daring to be outdoors on the beach. As I tossed a football with my sons—my boys can play football or Wiffle Ball twenty-four hours straight if we let them—my middle son looked at the Grim Reaper striding past and said, "Are we going to die, Dad?"

"Only if your mom kills you because school isn't open and you guys won't listen to her when she tries to teach you," I said.

Like many parents, we struggled with what to tell our kids about Covid and what was going on in the country. Early on, I had all three of our boys sit around the table and explained the data on Covid, the fact that they were probably going to get it and that we probably were, too, but that they would almost certainly be 100 percent fine if they got it.

As a result, our kids thrived during Covid lockdowns and weren't scared at all. (In fact, my middle son, as 2020 ended, would even say, "This was the greatest year ever, Dad. I wish it wasn't ending." I asked him why he felt that way. "You and Mom were home all the time and we didn't have school for months. What could be better?!" he exclaimed.)

My wife gamely did her best to teach our kids and I worked pretty much every day like normal.

I was already furious about the fact that our government was attempting to decide which businesses were essential and non-essential in the first place—all businesses are essential to the people who run them and their employees. How in the world were we at this place?

Even more than three years after Covid lockdowns began,

I'm still angry about what Democrats did to us and I bet you are as well.

The 2024 election won't entirely be about Covid, but there should be a reckoning for Democrats who made the worst public policy decisions of our lifetime. If democracy means anything at all, it should mean that politicians pay the price when they make poor choices.

Now, to be fair, Republicans weren't perfect in the earliest days of Covid, either. In retrospect we should have never shut down our economy at all, in any way—fifteen days to stop the spread was a complete and total failure—and we should never have shut down schools, either. But the Biden administration took Covid authoritarianism to another level. Never in any of our lives has the government reached out and commandeered more of our freedom than what the Biden administration did in the name of Covid.

As I said earlier, Covid crystallized my decision to become a Republican.

Because never in my life has one political party gotten more wrong on such a major issue. I firmly believe that within a decade, just like happened with Vietnam, almost no one will admit to ever having supported Covid lockdowns and school shutdowns. All of the people with masks on in their profiles who lectured you about wearing a mask to protect everyone will pretend this never happened. All the teachers who refused to work for years—while receiving their full pay—and led to the creation of the oxymoronic "remote school" option will pretend this never happened, either.

Already Democrats are attempting to execute a *Men in Black*–style memory block erasure of the Covid era in our country. The common talking point is that no one knew any better than lock-downs. But that is a lie. Many of us did. And, remarkably, it appears many Republicans are allowing this narrative to succeed, for there to be no consequences for all the Democrat failures on Covid.

Not on my watch.

Covid is a perfect distillation of what happens when Democrats have complete control of the government. The combination of a Democrat president, a Democrat Congress, and the collusion between those entities and the big tech companies created the most chilling authoritarianism of any of our lives. It turns out that every dictatorial move Democrats told you Donald Trump would adopt, Joe Biden actually did instead.

Remember, if Trump had ever wanted to be a dictator, Covid gave him and Republicans more of an excuse to do so than most presidents have ever received. Yet when faced with an unprecedented opportunity to undertake national powers the likes of which no president in our lifetime has ever had, what did Trump do? He mostly deferred to state and local governments and let them make decisions about what to do under federalism principles.

Never before has your state governor been more important. If you lived in Florida and Ron DeSantis was your governor, Covid disrupted your life on a minimal level. If you lived in California and Gavin Newsom was your governor, Covid took over your life (unless you were Newsom yourself and had an opportunity to eat at a fancy restaurant like the French Laundry).

There is a strong argument to be made that Florida in 2018 was the single most important gubernatorial election of our life-times. DeSantis narrowly beat Andrew Gillum by just over 30,000 votes, 4,076,186 to 4,043,723, or 49.6 percent to 49.2 percent. If Gillum had won, make no mistake about it, he would have shut down Florida just like California and New York were. That's bad enough for anyone in Florida, but I seriously doubt how many Republican governors in large states would have had the courage to make the decisions DeSantis made if DeSantis hadn't been out in front to take the brunt of the national media's criticism. Remember how Democrats tried to label him "DeathSantis" on social media?

DeSantis was rewarded for his leadership in the 2022 election when he turned a 30,000-vote victory margin into a 1.6 million margin. A .4 percent win in 2018 became a nearly 20 percent win in 2022, the largest governor's race win in Florida Republican Party history. And there wasn't just a victory in the election. The state went from having 257,175 more Democrat voters in 2018, the year of DeSantis's election, to Republicans having a registration advantage of 394,830 in January 2023, a swing of 652,005 in Republicans' favor in the space of four years. It's not just that DeSantis won big: he's probably made Florida a red state for the next generation or more.

In times of crisis, political parties and their leaders reveal themselves. In Covid, Democrats showed themselves to be tinpot dictators who would use any excuse they could to implement draconian power grabs and take away the individual freedoms of citizens.

So let's focus for a moment on the failures of Biden when it came to Covid.

Here is a rough encapsulation of the lies we were told that later proved to be untrue. We were told Covid didn't come from a Chinese lab leak, but it did, as the FBI and the Department of Energy now agree; that it wasn't safe for our kids to attend school in person; that masks would stop the spread of Covid; that six feet of social distancing would stop the spread of Covid; that you should Lysol your mail and groceries; that if you went to a store you must walk up and down the aisles in one direction to avoid the virus; that if you took an elevator you should turn backward and face the wall while standing in socially distanced shoeprints; that if you were outside in a public park you could only sit inside a taped circle; that if you went into a restaurant you had to wear a mask in order to walk to your table, but could then take off your mask and eat; that if you were on an airplane or in an airport you had to wear a mask, except for when you were eating or drinking; that if you got a Covid shot you would neither get nor spread Covid ever again; and that if you refused to get the Covid shot you would face a winter of death in 2021.

All of these were lies.

Every. Single. One.

But let's focus in particular on the Covid shot. (I call it a Covid shot in this book because, as I said earlier, it is not a vaccine. A vaccine, before they changed the definition, kept you from getting or spreading the virus you'd been vaccinated for. The Covid shot does neither of these things.)

First, the news that there was going to be a Covid shot available was suppressed until just after the 2020 election. It was one of many things that were done to keep Trump from being reelected in 2020. I've already discussed how Republicans should approach discussing the 2020 election in this book, but suffice it to say the rig job was in effect. If the news media had simply allowed news of the coming Covid shot and the Hunter Biden laptop story to be freely shared, I believe that even with all the other shenanigans Trump would have won reelection comfortably in 2020.

As I've told you, elections are about the future, but explaining the past can give you a window into what parties will do when they have power. The degree to which Democrats and their supporters stripped individual freedoms from citizens during Covid is unmatched by any moment in our lives. And if they get the chance to do it again, they will.

I got Covid for the first time, at least that I know of, in November 2020, just before Thanksgiving, probably at my gym, where many people tested positive around this same time. Since I work from home, I didn't miss a single day of work and Covid, for me, was at worst a light cold.

The next spring, when the Covid shot became available to people of my age in Tennessee, I wasn't in a hurry to get it because I'd already had Covid and knew I had natural immunity, which many studies have shown is at least as good at protecting you from Covid going forward as the shot. But my wife encouraged me to get it, so I told her I would, but only the Johnson & Johnson one-shot version and only when I was guaranteed zero wait for the shot. (I hate all lines and all traffic. I have many flaws, but one of my worst is I'm incredibly impatient.)

My wife made the one-shot appointment for me at Publix and, unbelievably, on the day I was scheduled to go, they pulled the J&J shot off the market due to adverse reactions. On the exact day I was scheduled to get it!

I never let my wife reschedule me.

I got Covid a second time, this time the Omicron version,

in January 2022—I know because I went and got the official test done so I could talk about the experience on radio—and didn't miss a day of work and felt pretty normal. Once again Covid was a light cold for me.

We have not gotten our kids the Covid shot because based on the fact my wife and I have both had Covid, we are confident they've had it, too. I'm not sharing all this information because I'm trying to tell any of you what to do with your own health decisions, but because I want to be as transparent as possible before I really tee off on our government for the most inexcusable leadership decisions of my life.

(I should also point out that based on risk profiles, I encouraged my parents, who are both over seventy-five years old, to get their initial Covid shots. But as the boosters have piled up and it's become clear the Covid shot provides, at best, a very limited protection for a very limited period of time, I haven't pushed them to continue to get boosted. They're adults, they can make their own decisions. But the data reflects that the Covid booster shots are mostly worthless after a few months as well, especially if you've already had Covid, as most of us have. The data also reflects that most Americans have come to the same conclusion. Just 17 percent of eligible Americans have gotten the most recent Covid booster shot, meaning 83 percent, a huge majority, essentially recognize that the shots are pretty much worthless.)

A bit earlier I gave you a small collection of the lies that were told about the necessity for Covid lockdowns. Now let me give you a roster of the lies we were told about the Covid shot. We were first told that if you got the shot you would neither get nor spread Covid. That was the entire basis for getting the shot. That's what President Biden, Dr. Fauci, Centers for Disease Control and Prevention (CDC) director Rochelle Walensky, all of them, got in front of the cameras and explicitly told us—that if you got the Covid shot you wouldn't get or spread the virus.

That's been proven to be a 100 percent lie, too.

When it became clear that they couldn't keep that lie going any longer, they changed their story to argue that the Covid shot would keep you from getting very sick or needing to be hospitalized. That also proved to be a lie, as many people with Covid shots were hospitalized. So next they argued that the shot would keep you from dying.

Again, that was a lie. Many people who got the Covid shot and the Covid boosters have gone on to die. In fact, the majority of people dying with Covid have now had the Covid shot and been boosted.

Their final argument is that it offers you some small measure of protection, that it's essentially the flu shot and you will need to get it every year for the rest of your life. That's all well and good, but the big problem here is that the flu shot has never been mandated by the federal government for anyone, and the flu shot often doesn't work very well at all.

Despite the fact that the Covid shot didn't work, Joe Biden attempted to use his presidential power to mandate it for tens of millions of Americans via Occupational Safety and Health Administration (OSHA) regulations. Biden attempted to legally mandate that every employee in the country, essentially, get the shot. He then argued that we didn't have a Covid pandemic, we just had a Covid pandemic of the unvaccinated. Finally, Biden channeled *Game of Thrones* and told us in the winter of 2021 that those of us who refused to get the Covid shot would experience a "winter of death."

All of these things were untrue.

As I write this, all of this has been disproven and now people with and without the Covid shot are virtually indistinguishable in terms of outcomes. Most parents have finally realized the data on the Covid shot and are choosing not to get it for their children. Also, there is substantial evidence that the Covid shot might actually cause far more risk in young healthy men, particularly with myocarditis, than any protection it provides.

I am still furious at what our government, almost overwhelmingly made up of Democrat politicians on a city, state, and federal level, did to all of us. In particular, the decision to shut down schools remains the single most indefensible political decision of my life. The decision to make kids wear masks for years, even after our schools reopened, was also indefensible.

We're fortunate that schools in our area of Tennessee reopened in person by August 2020. Most public school kids didn't have this good fortune. The oxymoronic concept of "remote learning" happened for far too many kids out there, for far too long.

I went to a wedding in the Nashville area in the summer of 2020. A public school teacher came up to me at the wedding and told me that he taught Advanced Placement (AP) history in rural Kentucky and that his kids had finished out the 2020 year at home, often with no access to the Internet. His kids were so desperate to prepare for their AP history exam that many of them were going to the only reliable Wi-Fi in their area, the parking lot of the local McDonald's, to be able to get their history assignments and study for their AP test.

And these kids were not alone.

We lost millions of kids from our schools during Covid. Kids who just stopped going to school because remote learning didn't work for them. Maybe their parents weren't there to ensure they went to remote school; maybe they didn't have reliable laptops or Wi-Fi. Regardless, those kids vanished from schools forever. They just stopped attending and no one was there to ensure they remained enrolled.

This hits home to me in a big way because I went to Nashville public schools from kindergarten to twelfth grade. I could have very easily been one of those public school kids showing up at a McDonald's trying to cram for an AP history exam. I was fortunate to finish most of my first year of college based on high school AP exam results. It's why I graduated from college in three years instead of four, which allowed me to save a substantial amount of money on tuition. I don't know what I would have done if my school had suddenly shut down before I could take those exams.

Earlier I talked about continuing to host my sports talk radio show even as there were no sports being played. But that wasn't all I did. I also used my show to fight for schools to reopen and sports to be played because I knew how important the return of sports was for normalcy in our nation.

That's why in the summer of 2020, I had to fight one of the biggest battles of my career. The Big Ten and Pac 12 were close to deciding it was too dangerous to play college football, and if they canceled their seasons it was believed the SEC, Atlantic Coast Conference (ACC), and Big 12 would soon follow suit. And if college football wasn't played, no other college sport would be played, either.

I decided right then and there I would fight harder for the playing of college football than I'd ever fought for anything in sports. Over the next several months, Outkick, both my radio show and the website, became the most aggressive media outlet in the country to support playing college football. Why was playing college football so important in my opinion?

First, the data was overwhelming that there was no substantial risk to young, healthy players. That was despite the fact that news outlets like CBSSports.com were running hyperventilating pieces claiming that if college football was played at least eight players would die because of Covid. (The actual number of athletes who died from contracting Covid because of sports? Zero.) But the most important data here was that if college football was shut down, many high schools wouldn't play fall sports and many wouldn't open at all.

I had regular conversations with Southeastern Conference commissioner Greg Sankey during this time. He told me that one of the biggest challenges he faced was how many southern high schools would shut down their seasons if college football wasn't played. As a public school kid who knew the importance of high school sports to so many in the country, especially to many kids who would otherwise just vanish when it came to schooling, I couldn't let that happen.

I made the calculated decision to go all in fighting for college football to be played. I was a maniac about it, pulling every political lever I could to influence governors on the issue, and I aggressively used my two biggest platforms, Outkick and my national sports radio morning show, to that end. I got every governor with an SEC, ACC, or Big 12 school in his state I could on the air. We'd never had governors on the radio show before, but I had our staff reach out to all of them in an effort to get them on to publicly support the return of sports.

We had Florida governor Ron DeSantis on several times. DeSantis was important because he said that not only did the SEC and ACC schools in his state need to play football, but so did every high school. We also hosted Tennessee governor Bill Lee, Georgia governor Brian Kemp, Mississippi governor Tate Reeves, Texas governor Greg Abbott, and Oklahoma governor Kevin Stitt. We put together an entire coalition of red state governors who would all come out in favor of college football being played in their states.

Each of these governors—all with ACC, SEC, and Big 12 schools in their states—came on and endorsed the idea of playing college football in the fall. Each time I would get a governor to publicly endorse playing, I would text Greg Sankey, the SEC's commissioner, and let him know we had another political supporter keeping the dream of playing the season alive.

I can't impress upon you enough, by the way, how much I came to respect Sankey. Under immense pressure from the sports media—almost all of whom were convinced the season had to be canceled because it wasn't safe to play—he stayed calm and reasonable.

Early on in the Covid era, I even called Sankey and told him that he was used to sports media being in favor of sports, but that wasn't going to be the case now. "You need to tell every president and school athletic director what's coming. They're going to get ripped to the high heavens for even considering playing. Get them ready."

I wasn't just lobbying to get governors on to endorse playing college football. I also worked as hard as I could to get the biggest asset of all, President Donald Trump, on my radio show to call for sports being played, too. Years ago, when Trump was elected, I told my wife that one day we'd get him on my sports radio show. I even predicted it on the air. Everyone laughed.

It didn't seem crazy at all to me, though. After all, Trump was a monster sports fan and we agreed on many overlapping issues of sports and politics, particularly as they pertained to getting sports back under way, which was an important signpost of a return to normalcy in the country.

Then, one day, it happened. After months of lobbying, the time was right for Trump to come on the show and endorse the importance of playing college football.

The night before the interview, when I told my kids the president was coming on the radio show, my middle son said, "That's awesome. He knows Vince McMahon!" (My boys are big WWE fans.)

I couldn't sleep the night before the interview. For regular listeners of my sports talk radio show, they all know our phones never worked. I mean, just complete and total tech failure all the time. My biggest fear was that we'd get Trump on the air and then we'd accidentally drop him. Or he wouldn't be able to hear us. In radio the tease is what you say as you go to break to try to encourage people to keep listening. That morning my radio tease was "Up next, the president of the United States."

That's probably the best radio tease imaginable.

Trump came on the show and said he 100 percent supported college football being played. But that barely moved the needle.

Later that very same day, the Pac 12 officially announced they were canceling their fall season. Shortly thereafter the Big Ten did the same. My stomach sank. After months of fighting, it appeared we were close to losing the battle for college football.

Late in that summer of 2020, after the Big Ten and the Pac 12 had canceled their seasons, SEC commissioner Sankey called me. "I think I'm going to have to cancel the season," he said. "The only reason I haven't done it yet is because I just can't figure out how to do it."

I encouraged him to hang out for as long as he could and keep up the fight. We just needed, I thought, to get the players to report to campus. Once they got to campus and started practice, and in the South in particular, where college football is religion, it would be nearly impossible to stop the games.

On Outkick and on the radio show we redoubled our efforts. I worked like a maniac, enlisting support wherever I could, fighting harder for college football to be played than I'd ever fought for anything in my professional career. Slowly, we gained allies. The parents of Big Ten football players, it turned out, were furious they weren't being allowed to play and filed lawsuits challenging the Big Ten's arbitrary decision to cancel the season.

For most of my career, I'd been an SEC guy, but suddenly I was the most popular media figure in the Big Ten, one of the only media members with a large audience who was willing to fight for football. (My buddy Joel Klatt, the lead college football analyst for Fox Sports, and I helped create a behind-the-scenes group of allies fighting for football. This book isn't entirely focused on Covid and sports, clearly, but in the near future I want to do a documentary telling the entire story of the behind-the-scenes battle to play the college football season. Because it's an incredible one.) Our crew was small, but committed.

As the football season inched closer, I began to work with the Trump White House, Tim Pataki in particular, to reverse the decision to end the Big Ten football season. We gained momentum, with Trump even getting on the phone with Big Ten commissioner Kevin Warren to try to get that conference to reverse its decision.

Heck, I was even involved in strategy sessions with the White House to figure out how to save college football.

But we still needed more allies.

That's when the players themselves, who had mostly been quiet, suddenly spoke out on social media. Clemson's star quarterback, Trevor Lawrence; Ohio State's star quarterback, Justin Fields; and many more players started a let-us-play hashtag on Twitter that went viral.

For months I'd been hearing from players, coaches, and administrators behind the scenes about how badly they all wanted to play, but they'd been afraid of being ripped to shreds by the sports media, who overwhelmingly had opposed a return to play for all sports and spread rampant fear-porn about the deaths that would ensue if sports returned.

Indeed, Mike Gundy, the Oklahoma State football coach, had faced significant censure in May 2020 when he'd suggested his players should return to campus and resume regular workouts. He'd been so vociferously attacked for sharing this opinion that many coaches stayed quiet, afraid of being swarmed by a mob on social media.

Finally, Outkick had public allies.

Slowly, thanks to steadfast leadership from SEC commissioner Sankey and the players speaking out so loudly, the SEC, the Big 12, and the ACC began to hold the wall.

We just needed to reach kickoff and have the games start. Because once the games started I was confident the parents of players in the Big Ten and the Pac 12 would force those conferences back to the football fields, too.

During this time, despite being the most likable and humble person in sports media, I made a lot of enemies in the sports media industry. People who had previously been my friends ripped me in public on social media, and in their articles they wrote about the impossibility of playing football during Covid. Negative articles about me and Outkick piled up. I've never been more attacked in my entire career.

But as I said when I started the book, my idol as a kid was Davy Crockett—be sure you're right and go ahead.

I knew I was right.

And if I'm confident that I'm right, nothing is going to stop me.

I worked hard, harder than I'd ever worked before. I drove the people around me, those working at Outkick, very hard, too, the radio show, everyone. I wasn't always the nicest version of myself. Sometimes I lost my temper with our workers and lashed out when I thought we weren't making smart decisions or things weren't being implemented rapidly enough. I was impatient. There was so much to make happen and it felt like everyone was against us and we didn't have enough time to do everything we needed to do to make the season happen.

In the late summer of 2020, every day felt like a whirlwind. I barely slept. I was on my phone constantly, running Outkick and all my shows and fighting to save the college football season with every ounce of energy I had.

The players reported to fall camp in the SEC, the Big 12, and the ACC. Kickoff inched closer and closer. In private conversations, Sankey held out hope with me that if smaller college games could kick off and then the NFL kicked off, momentum would carry through and everyone would play.

On August 30, 2020, the first college football game of 2020 kicked off. It was Austin Peay at Central Arkansas.

I watched every minute of the game, luxuriating in the return of football to television.

A month later, on September 26, the SEC kicked off a full slate of conference games. It was nearly a month later than normal, but finally, at long last, the season was under way. The ACC and the Big 12 also kicked off their games.

On opening day, I poured myself a tall glass of whiskey. I'm not ashamed to admit that when kickoff happened in the SEC, I cried. "We did it," I told my wife. "We really did it."

Not only did the SEC, the ACC, and the Big 12 play nearly complete seasons, but the Pac 12 and the Big Ten, under immense pressure from their own players, parents, and fan bases as the other conferences were playing, came rushing back to the field, too, even though their teams were only able to play shortened seasons.

And not only was college football played, but not one player or coach suffered serious Covid illness or death as a result. In fact, it didn't happen anywhere in college athletics. As I'd been arguing all along, football itself was far more dangerous to players than Covid.

Just about every high school in the entire South played football as well. We'll never know how many kids stayed in school because of those games, but I'm convinced we used sports to help ensure that millions of kids had as close to a normal 2020 school year as possible.

College football being played in 2020 remains my proudest moment in professional life. If Outkick and our radio show hadn't existed, I'm not sure it would have happened. When there were almost no voices in the entire country advocating for college football, we helped give the necessary space to commissioners, school presidents, athletic directors, coaches, and players to make the season happen.

There are many people all over the country who deserve credit for college sports being played in the fall of 2020, but I'm confident no one in sports media did more than Outkick.

So, again, I will always be immensely proud of what we accomplished.

And while winning the battle for football was a huge win, it was one of many battles I was fighting in my professional and private lives. While I loved college football, the most important job I have, and have ever had, is to be a dad of three small boys.

While my kids attended school in person in the fall of 2020, they were required to wear masks for all of that school year. I'm still angry that my kindergartner spent his entire first year of school wearing a mask all day long when it made absolutely zero scientific sense and offered him, as the data now reflects, no protection at all.

For the start of the 2021 school year many parents rejoiced because masks were finally made optional in our school district.

School, at long last, was nearly back to normal. At least it was until our school board changed the masking policy a week into the school year. You may have seen some of the video footage of the Williamson County, Tennessee, school board meetings. Parents showed up in massive numbers to fight the idea of masks in schools. As a parent of two public school kids, I spoke out against the mask mandate at my local school board.

Before I went to the board, I asked my then first grader what he thought about having to wear masks for another year in school. "I hate it, Dad," he said. "We all hate it."

So I went and argued as a parent against the mask mandate. I laid out the facts and data that made it clear masks made no sense. On the other side many health care workers showed up, mostly doctors and nurses, still wearing their scrubs from the hospital, to argue that if masks weren't required our kids would all be in mortal peril in school. All of these people spoke while wearing masks to further the cosmetic theater impact.

We lost the battle. Even in deep-red Williamson County, our school board voted to make masks mandatory. (They did, however, grant religious or health exemptions to any parent who requested them, meaning my kids, and many others, were able to attend school without wearing masks for the entire school year.)

But as I left the school board meeting that evening, I'd never been more encouraged. Finally parents all over the country were waking up to the assault on their children's freedoms. I called my radio show cohost Buck Sexton from the parking lot as I left that night. "This," I said, "is going to be huge this fall."

The mom-and-dad revolution swept Glenn Youngkin into the governor's office in Virginia and flipped the entire state from blue to red. The red wave was so strong, in fact, that it nearly flipped New Jersey from Democrat to Republican. New Jersey!

In the months and years ahead the data also came out confirming that parents who had fought against masks had been right all along. Masks didn't do anything to stop the spread of Covid. It was antiscience zealotry to require them in the first place. Masks simply became the MAGA hat of the left wing. While most in the left-wing media haven't covered it, we ended up with many test-case scenarios for the impact of masks in schools on Covid. In my home state of Tennessee, schools in Davidson County, where Nashville is located, mandated that all kids wear masks, with no exceptions. In Williamson County, directly south of Nashville, where my kids attended school, nearly half of the kids had exceptions to the mask mandate. What was the impact when it came to Covid cases in kids in the Nashville area? The two school districts had nearly identical rates of Covid. There was no statistical impact from the mask mandate at all.

That made complete sense.

Of course.

Because it wasn't like the virus could distinguish in any way between county lines. Yet on one side of the line, you were required to wear masks in restaurants, and on the other, things were perfectly normal. It was all complete madness. I'm still so angry about it that I don't believe I will ever live in Davidson County again. I expect to spend the rest of my life in Williamson County. I simply won't pay property taxes to Davidson County after their failed leadership.

But it wasn't just where I lived. In Los Angeles County there was a school mask mandate, while in Orange County, just south of LA, there wasn't. Guess what happened? Rates of Covid were nearly identical in these two counties as well. (Orange County, with no mask mandate, was actually lower.)

The lesson was quite clear: masks failed, and so had all our public health "experts" who told us they were necessary to stop the spread of Covid.

Here's how crazy things were even in Nashville. In the fall of 2020, I went to watch the Alabama-LSU football game at a local sports bar. (Yay, football! This was a game being played because we'd won the battle against the coronabros who had wanted to cancel the season.) The bar, because our mayor was an idiot, had to close by ten at night. (Everyone knows Covid doesn't spread after ten at night. Trust the science, moron!)

So those of us who had been watching the game at the bar left to go hang out and finish watching at a friend's house in East Nashville, just across the river from downtown. A little over an hour later, police knocked on the door.

There were fifteen or so people in the house. That violated the maximum number of people that could be allowed in a home and neighbors had called police to report the gathering.

The homeowner was charged with a misdemeanor violation of the health code. He was arrested and a mug shot was taken of him in his driveway. He was later sentenced to perform community service to make this charge go away.

And this happened in Nashville in November 2020!

Even in a state like Tennessee, the city of Nashville had so lost its mind that homeowners were being charged with crimes for having people over to watch football on TV.

I attended football games with my family in the fall of 2020, both in the SEC and in the NFL. Things were so antiscience that even outdoor stadiums were capped at 20 percent occupancy. In Nashville they—and I can't believe this really happened—zip-tied 80 percent of the seats to keep people from sitting in them and had ushers walking around to ensure that you pulled your masks up over your face between bites of food or sips of drink.

At outdoor stadiums!

(Truth be told, it wasn't all bad. My young kids had no one blocking their view, the parking lots were mostly empty, so you could park and walk in ten minutes before kickoff, and there were no lines for the bathroom or concessions.)

Chances are many of you have stories like this from your own life. We all do.

I bring all this up now because in 2024 we can't forget about all of this.

Democrats got everything wrong on Covid.

Everything.

And if democracy truly matters there must be consequences for these failures.

The mom-and-dad revolution of 2021 was real. It was palpable in a way I've never seen or felt political energy before. It wasn't Democrat or Republican energy, it was momma-bear energy. You know how you're never supposed to get between a momma bear and her cub? That's what happened with Covid and masking.

But that energy wasn't the same in America in 2022.

I think many Republicans let Democrats off the hook for their Covid failures. The reckoning didn't arrive in 2022 like it should have. Maybe that's because people were just exhausted from the Covid battles. I get it. Trust me. Few fought harder. But the biggest threat to democracy is when politicians make disastrous policy decisions and there are no consequences.

And so far just about every Democrat who failed the Covid test is still in power.

As I pointed out earlier, only one incumbent governor or senator lost in 2022.

There are many people out there who don't pay attention to politics every day. Many moms are at the top of that list. Moms—and dads—of young kids are super busy. I'm writing now, but a few hours ago my sixth grader came running up the stairs to tell me he'd missed his bus. So I loaded up my sixth grader and my second grader and raced them both to their schools. I'm about to leave writing now to go pick up my second grader at school and then I have to get my sixth grader to his football game and my second grader to his soccer game.

Somewhere along the way we have to pick up our ninth grader, too.

My point here is that if you've got young kids, every single day feels like a zoo. Everyone is running in different directions and your schedule is overwhelming and you're likely frazzled, just struggling to keep up with all your obligations. You might not be paying attention to every single detail in politics, but when it has to do with your own kids, you do. In a big way.

Republicans have to talk directly to these moms. They are all persuadable and natural Republican voters. Men—dads in particular—already vote Republican in massive numbers. But moms, particularly moms in the suburbs, are the swing voters who change election outcomes. If Republicans are going to win big in 2024, moms have to be added to our coalition in big numbers.

And they're ready to join up, they really are. I saw it with my own eyes when it came to the masking of their kids and the outpouring of what I called the Lululemon revolution. A yoga-pants-clad army took on the biggest powers in American government, and they won for their kids when it came to masking and the idea of mandating Covid shots for children. Families overwhelmingly moved out of blue states over Covid masking and shot requirements and moved into red states.

One of my favorite arguments to make over the past couple of years has been this: If blue states were really safer during Covid, wouldn't everyone have moved there instead of relocating to the red states? Look at the population data. Covid made red states redder and blue states bluer. California lost 700,000 residents from April 2020 to July 2022. Florida added 800,000 residents in that same time period. Wilder still? California gained population every year from 1850, when it became a state, until 2020. Then it suddenly lost hundreds of thousands of residents based on its Covid response. Included in those lost residents? California governor Gavin Newson's own mother- and father-in-law, who gave up on blue state lockdowns and fled to Florida.

And donated money to Governor Ron DeSantis!

I bet that was a fun family Thanksgiving.

No one was moving *to* New York and California, but many moderate/conservative (sane) voters fled those states. They were fed up with the Covid restrictions, and parents were the ones overwhelmingly driving those choices.

Florida, Texas, North Carolina, South Carolina, Tennessee, Georgia, Arizona, Idaho, Alabama, and Oklahoma all saw the most growth in domestic migration after Covid. All ten states are red. California, New York, Illinois, New Jersey, Massachusetts, Louisiana, Maryland, Pennsylvania, Virginia, Minnesota, Oregon, and Hawaii were the ten states to lose the most population. All were blue states in 2020 except for Louisiana. (But Louisiana had a Democrat governor during Covid, unfortunately.) In my own neighborhood in Franklin, Tennessee, there were no houses available because people from California, New York, and the Chicago area were all fleeing those blue state enclaves for red state freedom. Now, I know there's fear out there that these blue state refugees are going to bring their blue state politics with them, but I don't believe that's the case. I think we're going to make those red states even redder.

Indeed, that's pretty much what we saw in 2022.

Florida, in fact, is no longer a toss-up state. It's the foundation of the Republican Party now.

Driven by the moms, pretty much every parent decided not to get their young kids the Covid shot. Why? Because they did the research and realized how unnecessary it was. Republicans need to make this case to the moms in 2024, but we also need to tie this in with the biggest obstacle to many of these mom votes—a rational and reasonable abortion policy.

I firmly believe that Republicans lost many of these 2021 moms by embracing policies that were too aggressive on abortion. Moms should be Republican voters. Covid proved that beyond a shadow of a doubt, but you can't win moms in abundance without explaining your abortion policy and being reasonable.

I see these issues as deeply intertwined.

The right Republican nominee in 2024, the one who will win a landslide, will be able to persuade suburban moms that just as

Democrats were irrationally fearful on Covid, they're being just as irrational and fearful on abortion policy.

As I told you in the abortion chapter, moms don't want nine-month abortions, but they also don't want their teenage daughters being forced to have a baby. And you know what else they don't want? They don't want the government forcing Covid shots on their children.

Moms—and this is very important—WANT THE FREE-DOM TO MAKE CHOICES FOR THEIR OWN CHIL-DREN.

That's why, again, Republicans have to be the party of individual freedom.

If we do this, we don't just win: we win nationwide landslides.

CHAPTER 12

KNOW YOUR BIGGEST THREAT AND NEUTRALIZE IT

It sounds basic, but knowing your opponent is the essence of any playbook's path to victory. We've focused primarily on domestic battles in this book, but the single most important geopolitical foe in the twenty-first century, by far, is China.

China is America's enemy and chief combatant, and a Republican candidate who will win a landslide in 2024 must keep this in mind. Republicans must be a strong, vocal foe of China and be much tougher than the Democrats are. To be fair, that might not require being very tough at all. After all, Joe Biden just let a Chinese spy balloon traverse the entire country and did virtually nothing to stop it.

In 1984, a seminal film in many of our lives was released: *Red Dawn*. For those of you who aren't actual red-blooded Americans and either haven't seen or don't recall this film, shame on you.

The story, in a sentence is this: the Russians invade America and a group of high school students, calling themselves the Wolverines, lead the resistance to this Russian invasion.

Holy crap, what a movie pitch.

Take my money right damn now.

If you aren't standing up right now with your hand over your heart singing the national anthem, you're probably a Democrat doing opposition research on me by reading this book. Get out of here, you commie scum.

It's probably not a surprise to you that a film set in 1984 would feature American heroes and Russian villains, since this was a staple of 1980s American cinema, after all. But what may interest you is that they remade *Red Dawn* in 2009. Given Russia's comparative decline, the idea that Russia might be able to invade America was laughably absurd. There was only one country with the geopolitical might to potentially invade America by then—China.

So MGM made a movie where China replaced Russia as the villain. The soldiers were all Chinese, the battle flags were Chinese, the clear foe of America was China. But then MGM ran into financial difficulties and the movie was postponed for a year. During this year, early footage of the film reached China and the Chinese authorities were angered by their country being the villain in the film.

During this same time period, the Chinese box office had become a major attraction for Hollywood. Being released in China could add potentially hundreds of millions of dollars to a film's gross. MGM couldn't risk this gravy train. So with China angered, something extraordinary happened. All references to China were removed from the *Red Dawn* remake and instead North Korea became the villain.

Think about this for a moment. China was angry that it was the villain in an American film and its anger was so concerning to MGM, which needed the Chinese box office for many of its films, THAT THEY DIGITALLY REMASTERED THE ENTIRE FILM, TURNING NORTH KOREA INTO THE INVADING ARMY INSTEAD OF CHINA.

Now, Chinese authorities have long required American movie edits in order to allow them to be shown to their population. There are funny, and ridiculous, examples of this throughout the past several decades. The ending of the movie *Fight Club*, for instance: instead of finishing with a mass terror attack, it says that the protagonist was jailed for having mental issues. And different plot points have been excised for years. In a recent flare-up, the new *Top Gun: Maverick* movie, which featured a leather jacket with international flags on it, initially digitally removed the Taiwan flag in an effort to make China happy. Once an uproar began—what kind of pro-America movie was this, anyway?!—the film's producers relented, abandoned the Chinese market, and returned the Taiwan flag on the jacket in the film.

While we might not agree with the decision to edit films for Chinese audiences, films have long been edited for American audiences, too. Nudity and curse words are routinely excluded from popular American movies, for instance, so they can air on broadcast television and receive the lucrative re-air dollars.

So while remaining committed to artistic excellence and refusing all censorship requests makes sense as a matter of principle, most people who make movies have long since given up many of their principles in the first place. (I mean, these are the same people who gave Kobe Bryant, who was arrested and charged with rape, an Oscar at the #MeToo Oscars.)

As Ricky Gervais memorably said in his scalding opening at the 2020 Golden Globes, "If ISIS had a streaming service, you would be calling your agents." Most of the woke Hollywood universe is bullshit. It's all for show. But what happened in those few years to *Red Dawn* is illustrative of what began to happen all over the world—China stopped exerting control over just its own population inside its borders and demanded that the world acquiesce to its authority and dictates even outside its borders.

Most of American business went right along with it, without raising any issues whatsoever.

Hollywood's willingness to bend over backward for a communistic totalitarian country isn't particularly surprising, but the same thing happened in the United States with sports. Even before China unleashed Covid on the world, it began to insist on cultural dominance in sports, too.

Back in the fall of 2019, several NBA teams began their seasons in China. Before the preseason games commenced, Daryl Morey, then the general manager of the Houston Rockets, decided to weigh in on the battle for freedom in Hong Kong. He tweeted an image that read, "Fight for Freedom, Stand with Hong Kong."

China reacted with fury, banishing the NBA from state television and demanding that Morey be fired. The NBA bent the knee to China, apologizing for the tweet, calling it "regrettable" in a craven attempt to save its relationship, and its billions of dollars in contracts, with the country. Within days all Houston Rockets gear had been removed from Chinese stores and gigantic banners of top players were pulled down as well.

No NBA player, despite their woke politics in America, was willing to speak up in any way that might anger China. Indeed, quite the opposite. LeBron James, a great basketball player, but not a shining light of intelligence on any other subject, said, "We all talk about freedom of speech. Yes, we all do have freedom of speech, but at times there are ramifications for the negative that can happen when you're not thinking about others, and you're only thinking about yourself."

Before I continue with LeBron's quotes, let's pause here and contemplate that LeBron accused Morey, *who spoke out in defense of the freedoms of the people of Hong Kong*, of thinking only about himself.

It just got worse from there.

"I don't want to get into a word or sentence feud with Daryl Morey," LeBron said, "but I believe he wasn't educated on the situation at hand, and he spoke, and so many people could have been harmed, not only financially, but physically. Emotionally. Spiritually. So just be careful what we tweet and what we say, and what we do. Even though yes, we do have freedom of speech, but there can be a lot of negative that comes with that, too."

Why would LeBron decide to endorse China and essentially repudiate American values?

Money.

At the time of these comments James was making *Space Jam: A New Legacy*, a sequel to the 1996 film starring Michael Jordan, and he was hoping that China would allow his movie to be released there. If James said anything negative about China, that would become far less likely.

So he bent over backward to rip an American for endorsing free speech in China. Ultimately it didn't matter anyway, because China refused to allow James's stupid movie to be released in their country.

The result?

Lebron's version of *Space Jam* lost tens of millions of dollars for Warner Bros. Pictures and was almost universally panned by critics. In yet another kick in the teeth to LeBron, it failed to even come close to equaling the Michael Jordan version. The original grossed an inflation-adjusted $470 million, while LeBron's version grossed just $163.7 million. So LeBron's movies perform about as well relative to Jordan's movies as his basketball games do, producing roughly a third of the audience.

James's comments are jaw-dropping in their stupidity, but they are, sadly, reflective of the larger context that represents how American big business deals with China: there's a complete abdication of American values and a total embrace of Chinese values. That is, put simply, China's goal.

I bring up these examples from both film and sports because the story is important—as China's markets became more lucrative, China learned American business had no backbone.

We've also learned that China opening its markets didn't liberalize China and make it more like the rest of the world. Instead China insists that the rest of the world be more like it. The initial goal of American foreign policy as it pertained to China was to open up Chinese markets for American products. Then, as China enmeshed itself in a globalized world, it would become more like America, embracing capitalistic values en route to a freer and more prosperous world. But that policy failed.

Instead of China becoming more like America, America has become more like China. Instead of America exporting democracy to the Chinese, the Chinese have exported authoritarianism to our shores.

Let me use the Internet as an example.

In China, their authoritarian, communist government determines what can and cannot be read on the Internet by their citizens. It's incredibly common for a subject to simply be prohibited from public discussion. Even today in China, for instance, you can't look up Tiananmen Square to see or read about the brave protesters who stood up for democracy in Beijing on June 4, 1989. The death of hundreds, if not thousands, of democracy protesters in China has simply been erased from government records by Chinese censors.

The same thing is true of countless individuals who have run afoul of Chinese government dictates. Try to look up the sexual assault allegations levied by women's tennis player Peng Shuai against a prominent Chinese Communist Party official and you won't find any news of it in China. Even Winnie-the-Pooh, who has often been compared aesthetically to Chinese president Xi Jinping, has been censored.

As we discussed above, the Houston Rockets had all of their gear stripped from Chinese shelves and their games were pulled off television in the country the moment their general manager expressed support for Hong Kong democracy. Good luck trying to refer to Taiwan independence or mentioning anything having to do with Tibet's freedoms, either.

Indeed, WWE wrestler turned movie star John Cena recently had to apologize to China for saying in an interview promoting his newest movie, *F9*, aka *Fast and Furious 9*, "Taiwan is the first country to watch *Fast and Furious 9*."

China was furious when they saw the quote because Cena had acknowledged the truth: Taiwan was an independent country. China then demanded that Cena record a message in Chinese and apologize to the Chinese people for daring to truthfully refer to Taiwan as a country. Which, amazingly, Cena did. "I must say right now, it's very, very, very, very, very, very important. I love and respect China and Chinese people. I'm very, very sorry for my mistake."

Why did Cena make this public apology? Because otherwise China wouldn't allow his movie to be released there.

The Chinese government, by virtue of its control, simply erases any discussion of any topic that runs afoul of their world-view. They call this massive government censorship the Great Firewall. Most of you reading about this find that degree of government power chilling.

Because even in our divided twenty-first-century country, most Americans agree that the US government shouldn't be determining what we can or cannot say online and what we can and cannot see. And if that was occurring, at least for the moment, our own courts would prohibit that kind of government censorship as a direct infringement of our First Amendment rights.

But it's important to recognize what's going on here—we're

protected only from government censorship by the First Amendment. We aren't protected from private company censorship by it. So what our government has done, and it has only accelerated since Joe Biden was elected to office, is demand big tech companies censor speech they don't like.

That's the biggest revelation from the Twitter Files released by Elon Musk. Our government has been colluding with big tech companies and their friends in big media to rig our national conversation and our national debate on many of the most important issues in this country. This collusion between Twitter, big media, and big government, the revelation of which we're receiving only because Musk paid $44 billion to buy it, poses the biggest threats to democracy in any of our lives.

While you and I may view this behavior as default state action, so far many courts haven't prohibited this from occurring. A good recent example of this is journalist Alex Berenson, a strident critic of the government's response to Covid, particularly government mandates for the Covid shot. Looking at the data, Berenson correctly deduced that despite the government promising that two Covid shots would keep you from getting or spreading Covid, they actually did neither.

Berenson frequently shared this data and argued against Covid shot mandates on his Twitter feed. This angered the White House, which pressured Twitter and other social media companies to shut down Berenson's account for spreading "Covid misinformation." How did the Biden administration define "Covid misinformation"? Essentially Covid misinformation was whatever arguments conflicted with government mandates for the Covid shot.

As we discussed in the last chapter, initially you couldn't

question school shutdowns or the efficacy of masks or argue that young and healthy people had no need for the Covid shot. These sorts of arguments were expressly forbidden, in fact. The government couldn't directly censor Alex Berenson's Twitter feed, but they could pressure big tech companies to censor him.

And they did exactly that.

Berenson would eventually win a settlement with Twitter that allowed him to return to the site, but he was banned for more than nine months before that happened.

The larger context at play: America's government has begun to manipulate big tech companies in a chilling manner, to search out their political enemies and demand their cancellation while protecting their own supporters. What we've created in American life is a default Chinese wall on the Internet, managed not by our government directly, but by their big tech allies.

Even more chillingly, many of our nation's biggest media companies—the *New York Times*, *Washington Post*, CBS, NBC, ABC, MSNBC, and CNN—have refused to cover these unconstitutional actions undertaken by the alliance of big tech and big government. That means we've created an unholy triumvirate alliance in our country between big tech, big media, and big government, a default Chinese wall of silence that has curtailed our own people's ability to see what's actually occurring in their country.

This is emblematic of what America's interaction with China has created. Rather than making China more democratic, our government has adopted more authoritarian tendencies, cracking down on ideas they disprove of, ensuring that our own free press is under direct attack. Do you think it's a coincidence that Dr. Fauci publicly envied and praised China's ability to implement draconian lockdowns over Covid? Don't think for a moment that Fauci, if he'd been able to, wouldn't have locked you and me inside our homes and kept us there for as long as he possibly could.

Consider what happened when the Hunter Biden laptop story was released by the *New York Post* in October 2020. Our own FBI, which would later raid Donald Trump's residence at Mar-a-Lago in Palm Beach, Florida, at the behest of Joe Biden's Justice Department, briefed big tech companies that Russian disinformation was likely to arrive just before the election. The FBI, which had already had the Hunter Biden laptop for more than a year and knew it was authentic, and also had Rudy Giuliani under surveillance, (so they knew that he had the laptop's data as well and knew he was shopping it to media members), effectively seeded the big tech companies with the idea that the laptop was actually Russian disinformation so that, when the story emerged, the default response of every big tech company was the same: collude to stop the spread of a story that was damaging to Biden's election campaign. In my opinion there is no doubt that this unholy alliance between big tech, big media, and our own FBI rigged the 2020 election in Joe Biden's favor.

When two cultures collide, one often wins and the other loses.

Again, our belief was that by spreading American products to China, we would create a more democratic China. But we were wrong. Instead we've created a more authoritarian United States. Our 2024 candidates need to attack China for what it is: a direct and transparent threat to world and domestic freedoms.

But we also need to understand that China, to a large degree, has already succeeded in creating a more authoritarian United

States government. Yes, China is our enemy, but so too are many parts of our own government.

So far our government under Joe Biden has mostly genuflected at China's altar. If you doubt me, consider this: Barely a year after China unleashed Covid on the world via a lab leak, what did we do? We showed up in China and allowed them to host the 2022 Winter Olympics! We didn't even have the guts to say no to China when it came to permitting them to host the Olympic Games even after all their Covid lies.

And we're supposed to believe that the Biden administration would be able to adequately combat the Chinese if they decided to invade Taiwan? It was comparatively easy to ostracize Russia when they invaded Ukraine, but how do we effectively punish China for invading Taiwan when so many American businesses produce their products in China, we'd be risking a massive global collapse if we even attempted to withdraw from there? Indeed, the same global companies that shut down all their businesses in Russia would be unable to do the same in China.

Where do we go from here? I'm actually bullish when it comes to our long-range victory over China—as I'll discuss below—but our disposition has to change. China is not our ally, they're our enemy, the largest true enemy we have in the world. We have to view them as such. China should become what Russia was in the 1980s, a Cold War foe to be vanquished by American capitalism. How do we do that? We stand up to China and begin to point out their weaknesses.

Like the fact that Chinese power has probably already peaked.

Due to their disastrous one-child policy, the Chinese population has already begun to decline. The year 2022 was the first in which China lost population, at least according to China, in six decades. (It's important to be skeptical of all Chinese data. My one regret from March 2020 was believing any of China's data on Covid and trying to extrapolate that data to America. We know China lied about everything regarding Covid, including, in my opinion, where the virus originated. I believe, as do most of you, that Covid leaked from a Chinese lab in Wuhan, probably created there with assistance from American gain-of-function research taxpayer dollars courtesy of Dr. Fauci.)

Right now China has roughly one-sixth of the world's population, at around 1.4 billion people. Chinese women are having an average of just 1.15 babies each. That's despite the fact that China abandoned its one-child policy in 2016 and is now trying to encourage its citizens to have not just two children, but three. The problem with this? Most Chinese people don't want to have multiple children, because they've been conditioned over the past couple of generations that one child is ideal. Many Chinese people also can't afford to have more than one child because the standard of living in China is still quite low. Plus, there are far more men than women of childbearing age thanks to abundant abortions of girl babies when families could have only one child.

That makes the population forecasts even more dire for the decades ahead.

China's working-age population has already peaked, likely a decade ago. This means there will be a rapid increase in the elderly population, and demographic data reflects that the overall population as a whole is likely to be cut in half over the next eighty years.

The point of all this?

China's power and influence, contrary to some fears, have likely already peaked. But that can be dangerous, too; sometimes countries act aggressively as they weaken because they know in the years ahead they may not be strong enough to act. That makes the next several years particularly dangerous for Taiwan.

In the meantime, there's a strong analogy to be made between China and Japan. Those of us who are old enough to remember the rise of Japan recall that in the late 1980s there was abundant fear that Japan was going to usurp and surpass American power. That fear, chronicled in 1992 in the Michael Crichton novel *Rising Sun*, reflected a belief that Japan was buying up too many of the top American assets. But then, just as the fear peaked in the United States, Japan's economy stagnated.

Forty years later, many don't even recall the great American fear of Japan.

I believe forty years from now China could be the same.

Why? Because, and this is the case Republicans need to make in 2024, American exceptionalism and dynamism are real. There's a reason why the top companies in the world are founded here. But in order for that to continue we need robust and uninhibited capital markets. We need to embrace risk and the openness of our society and we need to ensure that Chinese companies like Tik Tok aren't allowed to do business here while China prevents American companies like Google, Twitter, Facebook, and others from operating there.

Freedom is the key asset in America, the one good we can offer that China can't match. But we have to embrace that freedom in order to unlock the creative industries and ensure that future companies are birthed here as well.

To do that we have to embrace creative thinkers. We have to unlock the skills of all of our people in a way that China is not willing to do because individual freedom ultimately scares their totalitarian leaders. We need a robust and uninhibited marketplace of ideas, yes, but we also need a robust and uninhibited marketplace.

Capitalism must triumph.

And it will, because that's the ultimate lesson of America: free markets follow free people.

Our other key battle with China comes from this fact: unlike China we are still a global destination for the intellectual first-round draft picks from around the world. But in order for that to continue, we have to fix our broken borders and fix our immigration system once and for all.

CHAPTER 13

RECRUIT WIDELY,
WIN CHAMPIONSHIPS

One of the great clichés of coaching is that it isn't the X's and the O's that win you games, it's the Jimmys and the Joes, aka the players on your team.

If you truly want to win, you sometimes have to add new players. In pro sports you do that through the draft and free agency, but in college sports it's still mostly recruiting, adding new players to your roster.

That's exactly what the Republican Party has to do, too. We have to expand our roster with new recruits in order to win elections. We have to get the right Jimmys and Joes. Substantial numbers of Asian, black, and Hispanic voters belong in the Republican Party. They're the recruits who can turn 2024 into a landslide.

Many black, Asian, and Hispanic voters are natural Republicans because they reject woke cultural arguments; they believe men are men and women are women; they believe in marriage, strong families, the importance of education, and hard work; and they are huge capitalists. They also, overwhelmingly, want strong borders.

Donald Trump's demand for a border wall was supposed to forever turn Hispanics into Democrats. Instead, the exact opposite happened. Why? Because Hispanics favor legal immigration and know the border has become overrun by the power of the Mexican drug cartels. Here's a crazy stat for you: Did you know that the Mexican drug cartels made more money smuggling illegal immigrants into the country in 2021, a reported $13 billion, than any American sports league made in revenue?

Just think about that for a moment.

Illegally smuggling people across our southern border was a bigger business in 2021 than the NFL.

It's madness.

Hispanics also understand that Democrats don't respect them. Witness First Lady Jill Biden referring to Hispanics as "unique as the breakfast tacos of San Antonio." Tacos, really! Jill Biden told on herself a bit with that comment. How so? The Achilles' heel of the woke white community is that deep down the reason they argue that America is a horribly racist place is that *they* are racist and don't believe minorities can succeed in this country.

The problem with that argument? It's just not true.

Did you know that, for instance, both Asian men and women substantially outearn white people in this country? In fact, the average weekly earnings for Asian people in the United States in 2022 was $1,496. White people earned an average of $1,111 a week. So Asian people aren't just making more than white people every week, they're making almost 40 percent more.

How would that be possible in a racist country? Is #yellow-privilege a thing?

And it's not just financial success that makes Asian voters future Republicans. In recent years Democrats have argued that our nation's top public schools, the most academically elite schools, aren't racially diverse enough. The problem? Too many Asians are attending them. In fact, Asian students are no longer considered to be minorities when it comes to college admissions because they aren't the "right" minority. That means Asian students are being directly discriminated against for being too academically successful.

The result? Democrats have argued that Asians need to be replaced in schools by black and Hispanic kids who score lower on standardized tests than they do. In fact, things are so ridiculous in this arena that standardized tests like the SAT and the ACT are increasingly being eliminated because Asian students are dominating them. This is fascinating because standardized tests were introduced back in the early 1900s to keep Ivy League universities, which were then filled by white Anglo Protestant students, from discriminating against Jewish students, who weren't being admitted. The standardized tests were designed to create a meritocracy so all students, regardless of their backgrounds or the school they attended, could compete on an equal basis.

Now Asian students, many of whom are the lower-middle-class sons and daughters of recent immigrants to this country, are being discriminated against at elite high schools and colleges based on their race. The Supreme Court heard this case in the spring of 2023 as we went to print, but the court seems likely to strike down affirmative action.

Indeed right now there is a revolution against woke school policies even in the uberliberal San Francisco school district, where Asian parents overwhelmingly rejected the existing school board members and voted them out. Why? Because while the schools were shut down for Covid, the board decided that schools named after historic figures like Abraham Lincoln needed to be renamed because they were evidence of white supremacy.

That's why in the 2022 election Asians moved to a large degree toward Republicans. This was most evident in Lee Zeldin's campaign for governor of New York. He won many majority-Asian districts and helped set the template for what a multiracial future the Republican Party could have.

So Asians and Hispanics are both natural members of the Republican coalition.

So too are black voters, especially black men. Black voters are increasingly realizing that Democrats don't offer solutions for the black community. What woke Democrats sell to black voters is the idea that white people are so all-powerful that black people have no potential for success, that their individual excellence and talents don't matter, that they are discriminated against to such an extent that there is no hope for success in today's America.

But this woke narrative fundamentally rejects the entire history of American life. It was only a few years ago that Barack Obama won back-to-back terms as president; Will Smith, pre-slap, was the most successful actor in Hollywood; and Oprah Winfrey was the most successful TV talk show host in history; today, the three highest-paid quarterbacks in NFL history are black, and Michael Jordan, LeBron James, and Tiger Woods are all billionaires. If America is so horribly discriminatory against black people, how is it that so many black people are the most successful in the history of their industries?

The truth is this: Republicans have an incredible message to sell to white, black, Asian, and Hispanic voters. They are the top recruits who need to be signed to help execute our playbook of dominance in 2024. America is the land of opportunity, the freest place in world history for individual excellence to be championed. All too often that message is being missed. Why? Because Republicans become too focused on their own form of identity politics—focusing on white voters without college degrees to the exclusion of appealing to black, Asian, and Hispanic voters.

Black, Asian, and Hispanic voters overwhelmingly have more in common with white voters without college degrees than they do with woke white people with college degrees. Republicans need to change their voter recruiting and ridicule woke white people, the kinds of people with pronouns in their Twitter bios, Ukrainian flags in their profile pictures, and three masks and a face shield when they take an airline flight.

The data is there to support this natural evolution. Since 2016, black, Asian, and Hispanic voters have been moving toward Republicans in a big way. According to data from AP VoteCast, in 2022 Republicans increased their support among Asian voters by 19 points!—from 23 percent to 42 percent in just four years. Hispanic support grew by 9 to 10 points nationwide, and black support for Republicans grew by between 4 and 7 points nationwide compared to the 2018 midterms. This is the beginning of a natural wave, a rebuilding of the Republican Party that is a multiracial coalition of people who embrace freedom and the meritocracy.

It's not just black, Asian, and Hispanic voters who are natural

Republicans; it's those who risk their lives to get to this country, too—immigrants. Joe Biden has been a disaster on all foreign affairs, especially the withdrawal from Afghanistan. One story in particular stood out to me there because I think it speaks to the power of the American dream to those overseas.

When America abandoned Afghanistan, Afghanis were so desperate not to be left behind to be ruled by the Taliban that they essentially stormed the Kabul airport, attempting to get on planes that they believed would take them to freedom in the United States.

In August 2021, Zaki Anwari, a member of Afghanistan's national youth soccer team, died at the age of seventeen. It's a tragedy anytime someone dies this young. But I want to share his story with you all today because it epitomizes what America means to so many people around the world. Zaki came from a poor family, but thanks to his relentless training and love of soccer, he had been able to make the national Afghan youth soccer team, and that roster spot allowed him to attend school as well. But with the Taliban coming to power, Zaki was terrified that his ability to play soccer for the national team and continue to attend school would be taken from him.

So he decided that he had to get to America so he could continue to play the sport he loved and pursue his dreams in a country redolent with freedom in his young eyes.

Zaki made it inside the airport amid the chaos of the American withdrawal, and as he saw a plane, one of the last to leave his home country, he sprinted alongside it and, being a good athlete, was able to climb up onto the wheel's support structure and hang on as the plane lifted off. Zaki was so desperate to reach America, you see, that he hoped to stow away in the wheel compartment.

As the plane climbed into the air above Kabul, Zaki clung desperately to it, trying with every fiber of strength he had to will himself to hang on, to survive the long, cold flight to another country, to America, where he'd have the freedom to pursue his passion, where he could play soccer and continue his education. But Zaki's grip in the wheel well failed him, and soon after the plane took flight into the Afghan skies, Zaki fell through the blue skies to the chaos on the ground below.

Zaki Anwari was just seventeen years old when he lost his life.

His dream? To be able to play soccer and go to school in America.

For that he was willing to risk his teenage life.

How many of you reading this book right now have kids or grandkids who play soccer and go to school? A huge percentage, I'd wager. And if your kids are anything like mine, guess what? That's not their only dream. Going to school and playing soccer is a small part of what they get to do in America every single day. Zaki's most fervent dream, a dream he held so tightly that he gave his life for it, was just to be able to go to school and play soccer.

I hope all of you will take a moment and share Zaki's story with your own children. Because very few of us ever take the time to reflect upon how much good fortune we all have to live in America today.

This kid loved America, a place he'd never even been, so much that he was willing to try to hold on to a speeding jet climbing tens of thousands of feet into the air to get here.

He was willing to risk his entire life for just the chance to be in America one day.

How many of us would do the same today? How many of us would run alongside a speeding airplane, leap and grab hold of that jet, and somehow hold on as that plane took off?

Just for the chance of living in America.

That's the power that American ideals still have around the world today. That's the love we provoke from citizens of other countries, who will truly give their lives just for the chance to get here.

How many left-wingers do you believe love America as much as Zaki did? I'd wager that most don't.

A Quinnipiac poll taken in March 2022, in the immediate aftermath of Russia's invasion of Ukraine, found that 68 percent of Republicans and 57 percent of independents would fight for America if our country was invaded by an adversary.

That's not ideal, but it's a fairly substantial majority of Republicans and a majority of independents.

Meanwhile, 52 percent of Democrats said they would leave the country if America was invaded.

Think about that: more than half of Democrat voters would flee the country if we were invaded by a foreign adversary. That's an incredible revelation, but does it really surprise you at all? Why would Democrats, who have spent decades trying to tear down this country based on their belief that America is inherently racist and evil, be willing to stand up and fight for this country?

If you believe America is a racist and evil place, why would you fight to protect it? Of course you wouldn't.

I believe America is the least racist country in the history of the world.

No other country has as many people from as many diverse backgrounds all coexisting as equals under the freedoms enshrined in our Constitution. The most consistent and fundamental lie that leftists tell is that the United States is a racist country. Nothing could be further from the truth. If the United States were a racist country, why would so many minorities like Zaki risk their lives to get here? Why would huge populations in Africa, Asia, and Latin America, minorities, all of them, seek so desperately to become Americans if we were so profoundly racist?

Put simply, they wouldn't do so.

These immigrants *know* that America is the least racist country ever. They're putting their lives, and their family's lives, on the line for this reason.

They know this based on economic opportunity as well. As we stated earlier, Asian men and women are the highest-earning group of people in America today.

But it's not just Asian men and women. By their second generation, black immigrant families from Africa make far more money than the average black person in America. Within two generations the average African immigrant family makes more money than the average white family in America. If America were so incredibly racist, how would it be possible for black immigrants to rapidly earn so much more than white people who have been here for hundreds of years?

By the way, why do you almost never see or hear anyone make this argument?! By now you have all clearly seen how brilliant and successful I am, yet why am I the only person, just about, even making this argument?

That's why immigration, to me, is connected with racial issues in America today—the desire of so many immigrants of so many different colors to risk their lives to get here ends the argument that America is a racist country.

Republicans need to trumpet the financial success of legal immigrants, while also supporting the idea of ending illegal immigration in this country. We need a secure border, yes, and Republicans should continue to advocate for one—we should be hiring more border security and fewer IRS agents—but we also need to share the stories of legal immigrants because many of them are actually the biggest supporters of the American dream anywhere in the country and they directly oppose the racism story the Democrats are selling.

I'm sharing this Quinnipiac poll because one of the things that I think Republicans get wrong about immigrants is not realizing they all embrace American exceptionalism. They all want to be here because of our unique freedoms, unparalleled around the world. They are willing to risk their lives to get here, just like Zaki was.

Most of us—with the exception of Native Americans—had ancestors who arrived in America on boats. Yes, some came voluntarily and some came involuntarily, but all of us owe our good fortune to be Americans today to an incredible risk undertaken by people who traveled to this country at great peril to themselves.

Think about those men and women, most of them climbing on board ships to leave behind the only home they'd ever known for a new land, a place they were coming to based entirely on the hope that a brighter tomorrow awaited them. We all carry the blood of brave risk takers and fearless optimists in our bodies today.

That same bravery still courses through the blood of today's immigrants. I think sometimes Republicans make the mistake of presuming that immigrants don't have a commitment to the same shared ideals, of a belief in freedom, of the commitment to the ideals that make America the greatest country in the history of the world.

To freedom itself.

Pretend that you were born in a dystopian United States, a place where it was impossible to make a good living and you and your family struggled to survive on a daily basis. Then pretend that the country directly to your north, Canada, was a great beacon of opportunity, where you could make ten times as much money, be far safer, and raise your family with a far better way of life.

Would you try to go to Canada?

I would.

Certainly I would if I were young and a hard worker.

Now let's change the dynamic. What if the United States had Mexico's economy and you could make ten times the money that you can make today in the United States by going to Mexico. Would you try to go to Mexico? I think I would as well.

Many of you would, too.

In fact, the hardest-working and the bravest among us would be the people most likely to make that journey, because, after all, it's far easier to not take a risk, to stay in poor circumstances, to not climb on a boat and attempt to make a dangerous journey to the United States.

I went to school with many of these sons and daughters of immigrants at Martin Luther King High School in downtown Nashville. A large percentage of my classmates at the public school I attended were first- and second-generation immigrants. Their parents understood the value of education, and their children worked diligently to graduate with honors and attend top colleges.

This is why the story of race and immigration is also inextricably intertwined with the idea of the meritocracy. Democrats now believe *meritocracy* is a bad word, because the meritocracy doesn't look like what they want it to. The meritocracy is, in fact, often not white at all; it's Asian.

I had two Indian roommates in college. Both were first-generation American students. I lived with Krishna and Shekhar for two years at George Washington University. Krishna graduated in three years and went on to get his MD at GWU. Shekhar got multiple advanced degrees. Both are doing great as adults. Krishna, in fact, was a Republican voter long before me. He used to lecture me about why I shouldn't be voting for Al Gore and should have supported George W. Bush instead.

I was fortunate to get to meet their parents in visits to their homes. I've rarely met people who loved America more than them. Why? Because they knew the value of American freedoms. Far better, in fact, than most Americans.

Americans often take American exceptionalism for granted because we've always lived here. But if you live somewhere where freedoms don't exist, you look on in wonder here.

At Vanderbilt Law School many of my best friends were first- and second-generation immigrants as well. Many of these students were Republicans, too, again, long before I was a Republican voter myself. One of those good friends talked about his dad's arrival in New York City and how he just stood in front of an American electronics store, overwhelmed at the bounty of a country where anyone could just walk in off the street and buy a television, something most in his native India could never even dream of.

This same immigrant would go on to read all the Federalist Papers and support Donald Trump for president in 2016. Why? Because he believes in American exceptionalism. Indeed, no one believes more in American exceptionalism than immigrants. They know what socialism is, they know what autocracies look like. That's why Cubans and Venezuelans are some of the most reliable Republican voters in this country.

I wanted to share these stories because I think some Republicans still view immigrants as a threat to our way of life. I fundamentally disagree with that idea. Immigrants are some of the most patriotic lovers of American exceptionalism anywhere in the world. I think oftentimes Republicans, in focusing solely on border security, don't praise legal immigration enough.

We should want all the top legal immigrants from around the world. In sports the top draft picks are the most talented people in a particular sport. The NBA, for instance, drafts the best basketball players in the entire world at the top of its draft. These NBA players, the top draft picks signing the highest-value contracts, are called lottery picks. The NBA, despite its woke errors of late, has a huge international population. The best basketball players in the world flock here to play.

We should want that to occur on a larger scale—every year

America should draft the top intellectual draft picks from around the world and bring them here for legal citizenship. Legal immigrants are a vibrant part of our economy. They aren't a threat to the American way of life, they are a huge asset to our country. The Republican who is going to win a landslide election in 2024 needs to do a much better job of talking to all of them, because they really are some of the most patriotic among us.

Right now Democrats favor, for the most part, open borders because they believe that illegal immigrants are more likely to vote for Democrat candidates if they eventually become citizens. (This is also why Democrats want to be lenient when it comes to granting legal status to illegal immigrants.) But what if Democrats are wrong? If Republicans did a better job of speaking out in favor of legal immigration while rejecting illegal immigration, it's likely the case, at least if you look at the recent data, that the anti-American woke belief systems of Democrats would actually turn immigrants away from voting for them.

Yes, build the wall, but also make sure there's a large gate. Republicans aren't anti-immigration; they're aggressively anti–illegal immigration. Guess what? So are huge majorities of Americans of all political backgrounds. As I write this book, the lowest support for Joe Biden in the country on any issue is immigration. Just 25 percent of Americans approve of his immigration policy, according to a recent Quinnipiac poll. So how do we limit illegal immigration? Well, the best long-term fix, honestly, would be for Latin American countries to be much more desirable places to live, but, unfortunately, we don't have much control over that.

So what we should do is limit the incentive structures for illegal immigration to occur here. The first, and the single greatest incentive structure for people to illegally enter our country, is jobs. There are many fairly high-paying jobs in this country that Americans either can't or won't fill. In fact, there are 11 million open jobs presently and we have an unemployment rate of just 3.5 percent. Most people cross the border because there are jobs available that pay them more money than they would make where they presently live. The economic incentive of jobs is, frankly, almost impossible to eliminate so long as America retains a dynamic and thriving economy. That is why we need more legal worker visa programs in place.

The other major incentive, however, is birthright citizenship. Now, there are two types of birthright citizenship: one is by blood, the other is by soil. If you're the son or daughter of an American citizen, that is, if you're a blood relation to a citizen parent, you should clearly get American citizenship. But I don't believe we should automatically grant citizenship to anyone born in the United States, so called birthright citizenship by soil. That is, we shouldn't be encouraging pregnant women to specifically travel to the United States with the goal of having their children here so those children become American citizens.

Citizenship being granted based on the location of a citizen's birth is actually uncommon around the world. In fact, only thirty-three countries in the world have birthright citizenship, and almost all of them are in North or South America. Why? Because birthright citizenship was a colonialist ploy to encourage people to settle in the "new world." That might have made sense when many Europeans were afraid of traveling to the "new world" and losing their citizenship with their home countries, but it doesn't make sense at all in the twenty-first century.

The result of our birthright by soil citizenship rules is that many wealthy Chinese women now exploit it by traveling to America to have their children here. The result is our nation's foremost foe is awash in children of dual nationality, Chinese and American. If an American citizen traveled to China and had a baby, would that baby become a Chinese citizen? Of course not. Can you imagine the reaction if in the 1980s at the height of the Cold War, Russian women were traveling to this country en masse to have babies on our soil to obtain American citizenship? There would have been enormous outrage. Yet China is taking advantage of this policy and almost no one says a word about it.

Indeed, no major European or Asian nation allows citizenship based on being born in the country. The United States and Canada are the only members of the group of the seven most industrialized countries in the world to grant citizenship to anyone who happens to be born on their soil. Canada, clearly, has the large buffer of the United States to make ingress and egress by pregnant women across its borders far less common.

I don't blame any mother who takes advantage of our birthright citizenship by soil policy, but it certainly wasn't put in place with modern travel realities in mind. No pregnant woman could easily travel to the United States in the 1800s, when this policy was created. Now women, especially those with resources, can easily travel around the world while pregnant and avail themselves of this opportunity.

Many illegal immigrants who aren't yet pregnant are also traveling here with the intent of having babies in our country. These women know that once they have children here there is almost zero chance they will ever be forced to leave the United States.

Their children are citizens, so how could they ever be forced to leave the country, even if they entered illegally in the first place?

Again, this will be called a radical and racist opinion by many Democrats—although every opinion Democrats disagree with is now called racist. But I believe most Americans have never really given much thought to how abnormal our citizenship-by-soil policy is compared to the rest of the free world. Put simply, it doesn't exist in most of our cohort countries and it provides a substantial incentive structure for both illegal entry and illegal residence here.

Ending birthright by soil citizenship is a long-range plan that likely has many political hurdles, but it's certainly a debate that should begin now. It's one that the vast majority of Americans are likely to support as well when they come to understand the facts. One thing I'd continually emphasize: if you're convinced your opinion is correct, don't be afraid to voice it. Many people are persuadable, especially on issues they haven't spent much time thinking about. In fact, this is why the First Amendment's marketplace of ideas is so important: it's only through debate that ideas with minority support can ever gain the majority.

So what does an immigration policy look like for a Republican who wins a landslide in 2024? It's a robust defense of legal immigration, and all the legal immigrants in this country, with an emphasis on the necessity of protecting our southern border to ensure that illegal immigrants don't overwhelm the country. In particular, a defense of our southern border should include the fact that the Mexican cartels now have better control of the border than the United States does.

The Mexican cartels aren't just making exorbitant sums of

money off drugs; they are also making billions of dollars a year off illegal border crossings. Just about every single person crossing the border from Mexico has paid a cartel to help shepherd them. Those cartels are also using these border crossings to push across fentanyl in gargantuan amounts. That same fentanyl is also killing more than 100,000 Americans a year, many of them young. They had decades of life still to live when they were killed by the drugs brought in from Mexico.

I believe that minorities, whether recent immigrants or long-time residents of this country, are natural Republicans, especially Hispanics and Asians, as the data from 2022 shows. Go to war with woke white people, because when you engage in that attack it will force the Democrat Party to embrace them even more, further alienating Democrats from their minority supporters.

The Republican Party needs new recruits in order to win a landslide, and they're there for the taking because they have many of the same beliefs that my grandfather, and namesake, Clay Travis had.

CONCLUSION

My goal in this book has been straightforward—share a playbook of issues that will guarantee a Republican win in 2024. Not a close win, but a monster win, a win that changes the trajectory of America. As I said at the outset, I have a big goal, but one I believe is reachable. I want 60 percent or more of Americans to agree that their president is doing a good job. And the only way I believe that can happen is with a Republican president. Because as I write this book, just 32 percent of American voters even want Joe Biden to run for reelection in 2024.

In 2020, Donald Trump lost Wisconsin by 20,000 votes, Georgia by 12,000 votes, and Arizona by 10,000 votes. If 21,000 voters in those three states had changed their minds, Trump and Biden would have tied in the Electoral College at 269-269 and Trump would have won the election in the House of Representatives.

Think about that for a moment.

Even after the clear big tech and big media rig job favoring

Democrats was in effect, as I believe it was, if just 21,000 voters out of 156 million voters had changed their minds, Trump would be president right now.

I understand why Trump was furious about the 2020 election, and I believe he will run again in 2024. But the data from the 2022 midterms shows that Trump can't win swing voters if he focuses on 2020. The 2024 election will be about Democrat failures and Republican solutions for those failures. You can't control the big tech, big media, and Democrat collusion. You can fight it with every fiber of your being, though. You can point out the hypocrisy of claiming to care about democracy while subverting the will of the people through an unholy alliance between big tech and big government. Still, you have to expect that the collusion is never going away, and you'll have to overcome it to win any election.

But in spite of all this, I'm still incredibly optimistic. (To be fair, I get optimistic when I'm drunk. And you're definitely drunk if you're still reading this book.) Many of you may wonder, with all the slaps in the face from sporting leagues over the last ten years, why am I still fighting to return sports to a place of unity as opposed to politics by any other name? The answer is simple: because I believe in fighting for sports as they existed in the 1980s, the 1990s, and most of the 2000s, until the woke brigade lost its mind.

I believe that sports is an important battleground against the woke and that we are going to win this battle in the long run. It's one of many reasons I'm proud of the work we do at Outkick, which is now one of the biggest sports sites on the Internet. I truly believe that unless you fight the woke in all aspects of our culture, they will never stop attacking. I'm not willing to abandon something I love because I disagree with the decisions they're making. I'm never going to be the equivalent of the kid who takes his ball and goes home when he's losing a game.

By the time many of you are reading this book we are likely to be enmeshed in the 2024 presidential primary battlegrounds. I expect that Donald Trump and Ron DeSantis will be duking it out for the Republican nomination, but as we all know, anything can happen in politics, so maybe neither of these guys will even be running.

But regardless of who runs, the 2024 election has to be about the future.

And the future of America, I'm 100 percent convinced, remains incredibly bright.

I truly believe that our best days are still ahead of us.

How can I not?

My grandfather and namesake, Clay Travis, was born dirt-poor in Muhlenberg County, Kentucky. He dropped out of school in eighth grade to make a living. He never got on an airplane in his entire life. His father, my great-grandfather, spent his life working in a Kentucky coal mine and died of black lung disease. My own grandfather escaped a life in the coal mines and moved to Tennessee, where he worked most of his life in the Dupont factory in Old Hickory.

My dad and uncle were the first members of the Travis family to go to college.

Now I run a large media company, appear on television daily, and host the largest radio show in the country. I owe that to the opportunities my parents and grandparents gave to me. I'm living the American dream because of them, and because of this great country I get to call home.

I was only ten years old when my grandfather died in 1990, but he was a huge patriot. He flew the flag outside his house every day. I remember driving past his house on Dickerson Road in Goodlettsville, Tennessee, back on that gray day in January 1990 when we took my granddad to be buried.

My dad choked up beside me in the car. "That's the last time," he said, "he'll ever drive by his house with the flag out front."

It's true. My grandfather, the man I was named after, has never driven past the house again. But the America he loved is still just as powerful and true today as it was in 1990, when he died. And right now the grandson who he never saw grow into a man is telling his grandad's story, his own truly American family success story, to the world.

I'm getting to write this book because my grandfather dropped out of school after the eighth grade and worked so hard that my own dad was able to go to college. Because I had opportunities my own grandfather could only dream of, because that is the quintessential American dream, to provide for our kids and grandkids opportunities we didn't have when we were young.

Whether you're white, black, Asian, Hispanic, gay or straight, poor or rich, that's ultimately what binds us all: the dream of something more, something better, something American in full.

Years ago, before my grandfather died, when I was just a young boy, we were all sitting inside his living room in Goodlettsville. My grandmother, also from Muhlenberg County, Kentucky, was talking with one of her brothers, my great-uncle Howard Jackson. He was telling us about fighting in World War II.

Like many Americans of his age, Howard had barely left his home state of Kentucky and suddenly he was forced overseas, fighting Nazis, while he was still just a kid.

He'd been with General George Patton's army in Europe and he said that one day, as a young kid in the service, word had come rushing down the military line in France that Patton was coming and all the men should line up on the road to be ready for his arrival. So Patton, resplendent in his uniform and with his ivory-handled revolvers on his hips, had come walking down the line. He stopped in front of my great-uncle and said, "Son, have you gotten to kill any Nazis yet?"

My great-uncle replied, "No, sir."

Patton nodded and said, "You will soon, son, you will."

Years later, on a trip to Europe, I had the good fortune to stand on the beaches of Normandy and look out over the open ocean, to stare into the distance at the waters all those ships traversed and picture what it would have been like to come ashore on that sixth day of June in 1944. The longer I looked from those hills, from those German bunkers, the less I could comprehend how we ever took the heights above the beaches of Normandy.

"How," I asked our American-born guide, "did they ever take these hills from the Nazis?"

"I think about that every time I stand here," said our guide, "and the only thing I ever come back to is because they were Americans and they thought they could do anything."

Because they were Americans and they thought they could do anything.

How perfect is that?

And guess what? They were right: they were Americans, and they could do anything.

And we still can.

It reminds me of the way I started this book, by telling you my life motto, the one I stole from Tennessee's legendary Davy Crockett: "Be sure you're right and then go ahead."

I get to say exactly what I've said in this book because of the men and women who raised me, because they all fought to preserve our freedom, to ensure that this country is the greatest in the history of the free world. They did their part—they handed us the greatest country to ever exist—and now it's our job to ensure it stays that way for those coming after us.

I'm sure I'm right and I'm going to keep going ahead.

And so, I know, are many of you.

Which is why I have zero doubt that America's best days are still ahead of us.

It's still morning in America. And the sun isn't setting for a very, very long time.

APPENDIX

Testimony before the House of Representatives—March 13, 2021

On August 11, 2020, the president of the United States, Donald Trump, joined my morning radio show, *Outkick the Coverage*, to discuss, among other things, the importance of playing college football in the fall of 2020. The president was on my show for twenty-five minutes and after the interview we posted several articles related to the interview on Outkick, the website I founded and own, which is one of the largest independent sports and opinion websites in the country.

The articles were well received by our audience because the president advocated a position both I and my site had been supporting for months: the importance of sports being played despite the challenges of Covid, college sports in particular. At the time there was massive pressure for college sports to be canceled for the fall. Indeed, within a few days of the president appearing on my show, the Big Ten and Pac 12 would announce the cancellation of their fall sports seasons. (Those decisions would later be reversed after immense pressure from players, coaches, fans, and the diligent work of the White House to help facilitate the return of sports in the Big Ten.) Our site traffic soared on that Tuesday, setting new records as our news-breaking interview with the president of the United States reverberated across the media world.

But the next day—and for the next week—our site traffic crashed.

Why?

Because Facebook killed our traffic. Overnight our readership vanished on their site. We lost 68 percent of our Facebook users and 76 percent of our new users on the site.

Given the fact that the sudden drop in Facebook traffic was costing us tens of thousands of dollars, hundreds of thousands of dollars over the next month, our tech team at Outkick analyzed all the data to see what had changed.

According to our tech team nothing in our posting schedule or article topics had changed at all. The only plausible explanation for Facebook's sudden decision to restrict our traffic was the Trump interview. Because we'd featured favorable coverage of President Trump and his opinions on college football, Facebook punished us.

We haven't publicly discussed Facebook's decision to tank our site traffic in the wake of the Trump interview before because our business team said if we went public with their decision they would likely punish us even more severely.

The result of the lost traffic on our site was substantial— given we are paid based on the number of impressions our content receives, Facebook's alteration in our traffic after that Donald Trump interview cost us several hundred thousand dollars. In the weeks and months ahead, we tested articles with Joe Biden's name in the headline to see if there was any impact on our traffic at all.

There wasn't.

Only Trump triggered site traffic collapses on Facebook. And in the event some try to argue readers simply weren't interested in these Trump stories, this isn't true. Our site metrics proved that readers arriving from outside Facebook's walls consumed these articles even more than they did other articles on the site. This was Facebook deciding which stories their readers saw, plain and simple.

If we wrote too often and too favorably about the president, Facebook punished our site. If we didn't mention Trump very much, our site traffic grew. The power of Facebook was clear and their message was, too: if you post content we don't like, your audience will vanish.

This was a chilling lesson.

And a scary one, too.

We, a media company in 2020, had to make a decision about whether to censor our writers' thoughts and observations for fear we would lose much of our ability to be heard and to monetize our content. This is an abuse of power by Facebook, a sign that their unrestrained and virtually unchecked power to control what Americans see on the Internet is nearly all-encompassing.

While Facebook would likely blame their algorithms for this traffic collapse at Outkick, that's a red herring. Algorithms are designed by humans and the results are monitored. Facebook can make any site soar in popularity or crush their traffic.

And they can do it in an instant.

But it's not just Facebook. This is the power of big tech writ large. We are living in a new gilded age, where tech billionaires—maybe soon to be trillionaires—have more power than any elected official in the land. Facebook's Mark Zuckerberg, Twitter's Jack Dorsey, Apple's Tim Cook, Alphabet's Sundar Pichai, and Amazon's Jeff Bezos have more power today than Andrew Carnegie,

J. P. Morgan, John D. Rockefeller, and Henry Ford ever did in the earliest days of the twentieth century. These modern-day tech monopolists can pick presidential election winners, control our national debates, and decide whose voice is heard and whose voice is not heard. The Supreme Court no longer decides what the law of the First Amendment is in this country; these tech executives do. In practice, big tech controls the country.

And they control the country by deciding what you see.

And big tech's power is only growing in the wake of Joe Biden's election.

Just last week Facebook flagged an Outkick article based on an excellent *Wall Street Journal* editorial by a Johns Hopkins professor, Dr. Makary. Our Outkick headline was straightforward and direct: "Johns Hopkins Medical Professional: Herd Immunity Will Be Here by April." It then laid out the argument of the doctor and linked to the *Wall Street Journal* piece for anyone who wanted to consider his arguments in their totality.

We shared our own article on Facebook.

Shortly thereafter we received the following email from Facebook.

The subject line was positively Orwellian.

Subject: Important Notification: Misinformation Violation

Our thought crime according to the fact-checkers at Facebook?

We had shared an *opinion piece* that Facebook's fact-checkers disagreed with. Again, this was an opinion piece by a highly credentialed doctor giving his opinion on an uncertain future event. This was the second time an Outkick article had been labeled as misinformation. The other labeling occurred after we *linked to the CDC's own website* on Covid-19 data. The thought police at Facebook labeled both articles as violations of their site policies and our Facebook traffic collapsed by over 80 percent in the ensuing weeks, costing us hundreds of thousands of dollars once more.

We appealed both fact-check rulings by Facebook. The company never responded or changed their determinations, despite both decisions clearly being made in error. Not only was Facebook deciding what its audience could see, it was unwilling to provide any measure of due process when its fact-checkers erred. There was no appeal, no opportunity to be heard. Facebook was an information dictator, judge, jury, and executioner all in one all-powerful seat.

Facebook's message in both circumstances was clear: if you share opinions we don't like, you will pay the consequences. And in the case of media companies, let me be clear: the consequences are often direct and consequential when it comes to finances. Facebook controls the ability of many companies to make payroll and meet their business goals.

For many businesses, Facebook's market control, when combined with Instagram, is near complete.

Facebook is not a neutral platform and neither are most of the big tech publishers which claim neutrality.

Consider the power of Twitter as well to serve not just as a platform, but as an opinion-based publisher as well.

Several months ago one of our writers posted an opinion piece about women in sports media, specifically addressing the different standards of speech for men and women sports commentators. The piece received ample attention on the Internet at large, including on Twitter.

The day it was published the article went viral on Twitter's trending topics section.

The Twitter explanation of why the story had gone viral stated as follows: "Jason Whitlock opens himself up to criticism *after making sexist comments about ESPN hosts*."

This is not a neutral comment from a tech platform. Someone at Twitter, we don't even know who, decided to label his column as sexist against ESPN hosts. That's certainly an opinion an individual reader could have, but why should Twitter, which claims to be an independent tech platform, be making editorial decisions about what content says? That's not what platforms do, that's what publishers do. This distinction is important because Twitter argues it isn't responsible for the comments made on its platform because it's not a publisher.

But what about when they clearly exercise opinion-based editorial judgments, which happens all the time? There is no actual distinction in these cases between publisher and platform; they are one and the same.

The message from Twitter was clear: if you have an opinion we disagree with, we will attack you, labeling you as sexist. And this is something that as a media owner I see happening every day to countless individuals across the country.

During the election big tech companies colluded and conspired to keep the *New York Post*'s story on Hunter Biden's Chinese and Ukrainian business interests from being read and shared on their site. Twitter even locked the account of the *New York Post*, one of our nation's oldest newspapers. How is this anything other than a direct editorial decision? Twitter decided it didn't like the *Post*'s content and refused to allow it to be shared.

Tech companies colluded to ensure the story wasn't widely shared on their platforms.

Shortly after the election, Amazon Web Services shut down Parler, refusing to even allow the site to be hosted on the Internet. It is nothing short of a modern-day book burning, an incredible irony given Amazon was founded to provide every book to readers. Apple followed suit, banning the Parler app from inclusion on its App Store.

Effectively these tech companies had colluded to destroy the business of a company they disagreed with—I don't believe we could find a more chilling example of antitrust activity by monopolistic companies in our nation's media history.

But it wasn't just happening to Parler.

It was even happening, ostensibly, to the most powerful man in the world, the president of the United States, Donald Trump.

In January of this year, Facebook, Twitter, Google, Spotify, Snapchat, Instagram, Shopify, Reddit, Twitch, YouTube, TikTok, and Pinterest all either banned or restricted the democratically elected president of the United States at the time, Donald Trump, from speaking to the country on their platforms.

The tech companies were making it very clear: they were more powerful than our nation's democracy.

Just in the past month the United States Congress built on this big tech collusion by holding hearings demanding Fox News and other conservative networks not be carried in the cable bundle. Why are hearings like these possible? Because the big tech companies have set the precedent that if they don't like the speech, no one else should hear it, either.

We are now witnessing a potentially much larger collusion

forming between the big tech companies and at least one political party itself. But let's not fool ourselves into thinking big tech will always be on this one side. As the pendulum of society swings, so too will what they censor continue to grow. The digital book burning, in other words, is growing, not shrinking, in the wake of Donald Trump's defeat.

As a lawyer who owns a media company, I believe we have effectively ceded our nation's First Amendment rights to the titans of the tech industry. These monopolistic tech companies are so powerful—and frequently are working in such close concert with one another—that they can shut down any ideas that displease them and crush any companies that don't toe the line when it comes to supporting their practices. The result of noncompliance is a modern-day digital purgatory: either you stay silent in the hopes these tech companies don't notice your platform and substantially restrict your ability to run your business, or you speak out and the very foundation of your business itself is in danger.

Before I agreed to speak today, there was an internal debate inside Outkick. Should we or should we not speak the truth today, knowing that in so doing there was a very real chance these tech monopolies might take aim at us and attempt to cancel our business?

As the owner of the company, it was ultimately my choice and I decided to say what many media companies in the country are too afraid to say: it's time for big tech to be held accountable for their censorious and anti–First Amendment practices. It's way past time for more of us in media to speak out aggressively about the importance of America's marketplace of ideas and we can no longer allow the modern-day versions of the robber barons in early-twentieth-century America to continue to own our country's marketplace of ideas.

I am not a rabid partisan. I worked on Al Gore's 2000 presidential campaign, donated money to John Kerry's presidential campaign in 2004, and worked to help elect Barack Obama twice. But in 2020 I voted for Donald Trump, the first Republican I have ever supported for president. I did so not because I believed Donald Trump was a perfect candidate, he certainly wasn't, but because I care more about the robust and uninhibited exchange of ideas in our country than I do anything else. I am a First Amendment absolutist and I believe cancel culture intertwined with identity politics is the greatest threat to our country in my life.

This is not a partisan issue.

We must have content-neutral policies in the online world and we cannot allow big tech companies to pick and choose which sides they favor, artificially impacting the marketplace of ideas in the process. It's well past time that everyone—Democrats, Republicans, and independents—recognizes the truth: big tech controls our digital lives and they aren't being held accountable for that control.

Our system for online discourse is completely rigged and totally broken.

We must change that.

Now.